insight text guide

Justine McGinnis

Never Let Me Go

Kazuo Ishiguro

First published in 2022.

Insight Publications Pty Ltd
3/350 Charman Road
Cheltenham VIC 3192
Australia
Tel: +61 3 8571 4950
Fax: +61 3 8571 0257
Email: books@insightpublications.com.au

www.insightpublications.com.au

A catalogue record for this book is available from the National Library of Australia

Kazuo Ishiguro's Never Let Me Go / Justine McGinnis

Justine McGinnis asserts the moral right to be identified as the author of this work.

ISBNs:
9781922771322 (print)
9781922771339 (digital)
9781922771346 (bundle: print + digital)

Cover design by Melisa Paredes

Printed in Australia by Ligare Book Printers

contents

CHARACTER MAP

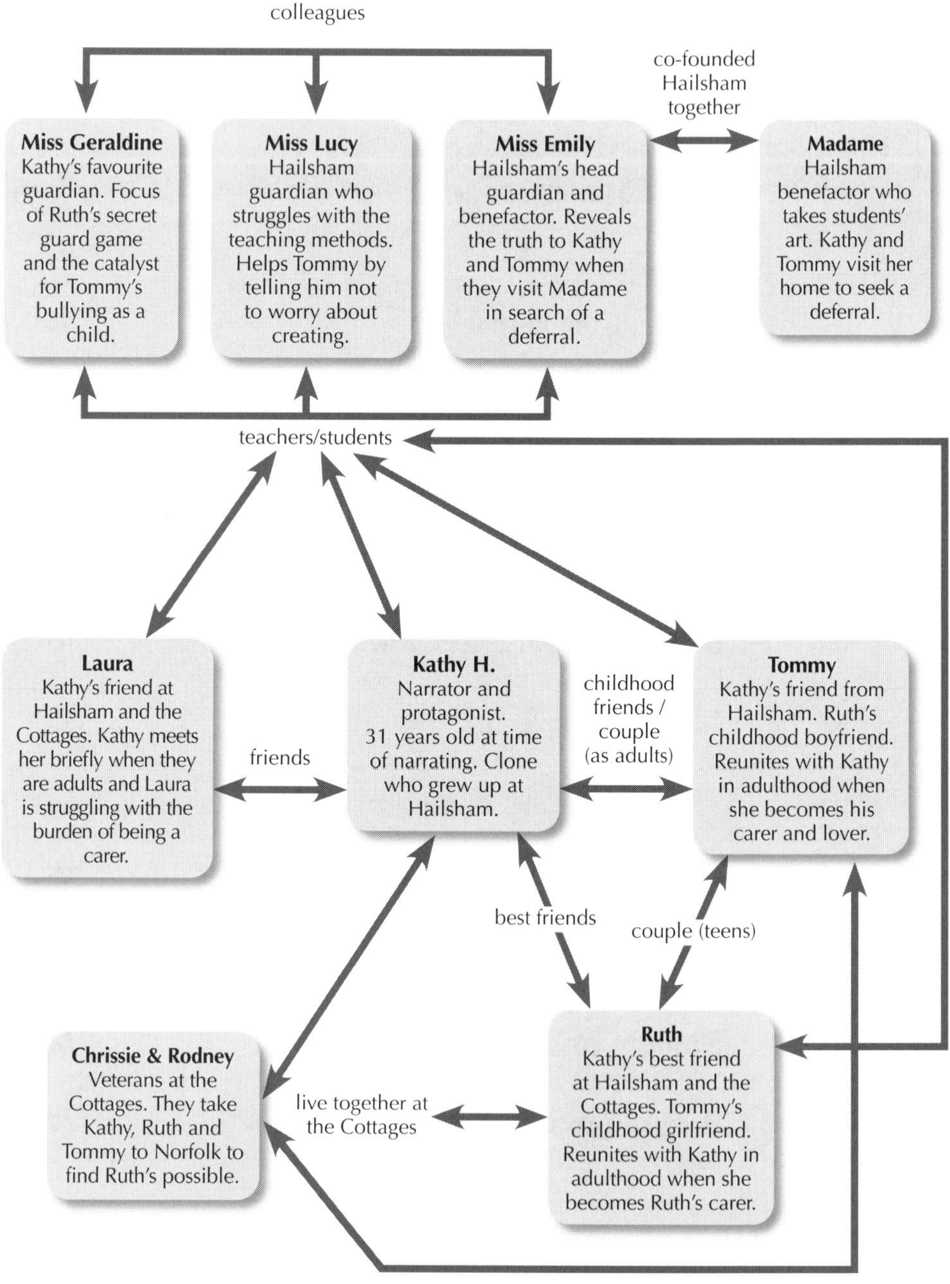

OVERVIEW

About the author

Kazuo Ishiguro was born in Nagasaki, Japan in 1954 and immigrated to Great Britain with his family in 1960 when his father, a research oceanographer, was employed by the British government. He grew up in Surrey and now lives in London. Ishiguro has a Bachelor of Arts degree in English Literature and Philosophy and holds a Master of Arts in Creative Writing. He worked briefly as a social worker before publishing his first novel, *A Pale View of Hills*, in 1982. He has written eight novels, which have been translated into over fifty languages, as well as five screenplays, numerous short stories and song lyrics for jazz artist Stacey Kent.

His most acclaimed novel, *The Remains of the Day*, was published in 1989, won the Booker Prize for Fiction and was adapted into an award-winning film starring Emma Thompson and Anthony Hopkins. *Never Let Me Go* was published in 2005 to widespread acclaim. It was shortlisted for that year's Man Booker Prize, and adapted into a stage play and television series in Japan, and a British feature film starring Carey Mulligan, Andrew Garfield and Keira Knightley. Ishiguro's work frequently features prewar and postwar settings, unreliable first-person narrators, dramatic irony and characters grappling with memories of the past. In 2017 he won the Nobel Prize in Literature and in the following year received a British knighthood for services to literature and the Order of the Rising Sun, Gold and Silver Star from Japan.

Synopsis

In a counter-factual 1990s England, Kathy H. has been a carer for organ donors for almost twelve years. Kathy and the donors are clones created for the purpose of organ harvesting. Kathy's time as a carer is coming to an end and she will soon become a donor herself. She narrates the novel in retrospection, reflecting on her life and relationships. Growing up at Hailsham, a prestigious boarding school for clones, Kathy and her friends live a seemingly idyllic life nestled away from the world and learn to see their futures as donors as a special honour. Students are taught to respect their bodies by maintaining perfect health, take pride in their artistic pursuits and follow rules unquestioningly. Their education is limited by a rigid curriculum and minimal access to information about the outside world.

As clones, the students have no families, so friendships are pivotal to their sense of self and security. Kathy's closest friends are Ruth and Tommy; however, these relationships are fraught with tension. Ruth is insecure and manipulative, while Tommy struggles to conform to Hailsham's expectations. Although Kathy's fondness for Tommy is reciprocated from an early age, Tommy becomes Ruth's boyfriend. The guardians, while caring and supportive, maintain a professional distance from the students. One of the guardians, Miss Lucy, struggles with the deceptive withholding of information about the students' lives and inevitable fate. She leaves the school suddenly without explanation.

At sixteen, Kathy, Ruth and Tommy move to the Cottages where they get their first taste of the outside world. Meeting clones from other schools, they come to realise Hailsham students are envied for their privileged upbringing. Rumours and fantasies about dream futures, possibles (the people from whom students were cloned) and deferrals (a concession allowing Hailsham students who are in love to delay becoming donors) create tensions and confusion. Kathy struggles to understand her sexual urges and her relationships with Ruth and Tommy become increasingly conflicted. After a significant falling out with them, Kathy leaves to begin carer training.

Years later, Kathy becomes Ruth's carer. The pair slowly reconcile their past, and Ruth apologises for preventing Kathy and Tommy from being a couple. They invite Tommy to join them on a trip to see an abandoned boat, during which Ruth reveals her desire for Tommy and Kathy to be together and seek a deferral. After Ruth dies, Kathy becomes Tommy's carer and they become lovers. They visit Madame, an enigmatic figure from their childhood, to request a deferral. There they find Miss Emily, their former Hailsham headmistress, who admits deferrals don't exist and reveals several harsh truths about the clones and the organ donor program.

Kathy and Tommy struggle with the reality that their romance is doomed. When Tommy receives notice of his fourth donation, he asks for a new carer, not wanting Kathy to watch him suffer a slow and painful death. After Tommy dies and Kathy's time to begin donations draws nearer, Kathy laments the loss of Ruth, Tommy and Hailsham. Standing at the edge of a field, she imagines Tommy and everything else she has lost appearing in front of her and is comforted by the memories no one can take away from her.

Character summaries

Kathy H.

The novel's protagonist and narrator. Grows up at Hailsham and stoically accepts the life prescribed to her. Thirty-one at the time of narrating the events, she has been a carer for almost twelve years and is widely respected for excelling at the job. She becomes Ruth's carer (until Ruth dies) and later Tommy's carer and lover.

Ruth

Kathy's best friend and Tommy's girlfriend. Fiery and manipulative, she is the natural leader of their social group but becomes subdued and remorseful as an adult. Before she dies, she urges Kathy and Tommy to seek a deferral so they can be together.

Tommy

Kathy's childhood friend and Ruth's boyfriend. As a child, he's prone to angry outbursts and is bullied for his lack of artistic ability. Kathy becomes his carer and they become romantic partners.

Miss Geraldine

Kind-hearted and popular Hailsham guardian. Young Ruth forms a secret guard to protect Miss Geraldine from an imaginary abduction.

Miss Lucy

Hailsham guardian who struggles with the teaching methods that deceive the students. Bolsters Tommy's confidence when she encourages him to not worry about his artistic struggles. Leaves Hailsham abruptly.

Miss Emily

Head guardian at Hailsham. Older than most guardians and a firm authority figure. Quick and intelligent but occasionally slips into a dreamlike daze. Tommy and Kathy meet her again as adults and she is revealed to be less benevolent than they had believed.

Madame (Marie-Claude)

Cold and aloof Hailsham benefactor who visits occasionally to collect students' best artwork. Believed to be Miss Emily's superior but later revealed to be Hailsham's co-founder alongside Miss Emily.

Chrissie

A veteran at the Cottages. Rodney's girlfriend. Is welcoming to new students but Kathy is wary of her motives. She's intrigued by and envious of students from Hailsham.

Rodney

A veteran at the Cottages. Chrissie's boyfriend. Thinks he might have seen Ruth's possible in Norfolk and drives Tommy, Ruth, Kathy and Chrissie there to look for her.

BACKGROUND & CONTEXT

Author's context

Kazuo Ishiguro was born in Japan and moved to England when he was five. In his Nobel Prize acceptance speech, Ishiguro reflected on his childhood, describing himself as having been happily acclimatised to the norms of middle-class British life while maintaining a connection to his Japanese identity through imagination and memory (Ishiguro 2017). This interplay of memory and identity is a common theme in Ishiguro's work.

Postwar and contemporary England

The novel's present is the late 1990s, indicating Kathy was born in the late 1960s and grew up in the 1970s and early 1980s. Descriptions of settings and references to details from that era such as cassette tapes, Walkmans (small portable cassette players with headphones), car models and television programs suggest the England depicted is identical to the real-world England at that time, with the exception of human clones and the state-run organ harvesting program, which, in the world of the novel, commenced shortly after World War II.

The end of World War II triggered devasting upheaval in the United Kingdom due to government debt and the loss of wartime manufacturing and exports. In response, the government nationalised many services such as energy and transport, and implemented free medical care and a welfare system. Over successive decades unrest continued due to inflation; industrial conflict; a surge in migration which fuelled inequality and racial tensions; the civil rights, women's liberation and counter-culture movements; Northern Ireland's armed violence and acts of terrorism; the reintroduction of privatisation; and a shift towards neoliberalism under Prime Minister Margaret Thatcher in the 1980s.

The fictional society of the novel aligns with Britain's context in many ways. The state-run donor program is plausible in the context of England's welfare and healthcare programs; the Hailsham project's reliance on political and corporate support aligns with the UK's open market economy and political system. The inequality apparent in the clones' segregation and the varying conditions in schools and recovery centres mirrors the British class system, which maintains a monarchy and where, despite increased social mobility since the Industrial Revolution, a small elite group inherits wealth, land and positions in parliament by virtue of birth. Assuming the actual events of the twentieth century are occurring in the background, the clones' ignorance emphasises their segregation. On one hand, they're free of the anxieties of social upheaval but, on the other, they're excluded from public discourse around racial, gender and class equality which could empower them to question their oppression.

Scientific progress and biomedical ethics

While cloning and organ harvesting are speculative elements of the narrative, the ethical concerns raised are pertinent to real issues. Miss Emily explains that the donor program originated in the 1950s during a time of rapid breakthroughs, and society embraced the benefits without considering consequences. This correlates with historical evidence that periods of intense progress elicit positive and negative outcomes. For example, the Industrial Revolution created new industries, cheaper goods and improved quality of life for many, but also brought pollution and global reliance on petroleum. World War II provided advancements in medicine and transport, but also the invention of the atomic bomb which the US detonated over the Japanese cities of Hiroshima and Nagasaki in 1945, killing hundreds of thousands of people, mostly civilians. This was followed by nuclear proliferation and the Cold War.

In the decade preceding the publication of *Never Let Me Go*, advancements in biomedicine and genetics offered exciting opportunities to better understand human and animal biology, treat life-threatening and disabling conditions, improve the quality of agricultural livestock, and prevent the extinction of animals. However, they also generated heated public and political debate. Common concerns included:

- causing harm to animals, given cloning experiments resulted in high morbidity and genetic abnormalities
- questions about when life begins, with many religious groups opposing the intentional destruction of human embryos in stem cell research
- moral repulsion and fears about violating the principles of nature.

Cloning

A clone is an identical genetic copy of a living cell or organism. Cloning research originated in the early 1900s with numerous experiments throughout the twentieth century. In 1996, Ian Wilmut produced the first clone of a mammal – Dolly the sheep – proving it possible to clone an animal from the cell of a living adult. This breakthrough expedited developments in stem cell research and generated widely publicised controversy. Debates reignited six years later when Dolly died an early death after suffering osteoporosis and lung problems. Concerns centred around animal cruelty and fears about human cloning. Currently, no one has successfully cloned a human embryo and attempting this is illegal in many countries. However, cloning human genes, cells and tissue is common.

The fictional society of the novel puts great emphasis on clones being 'copied'. The rationalisation seems to be that clones are not human because they're not biologically unique, and they're not a natural form of life because they were produced artificially. Scientific facts poke holes in these arguments. Firstly, clones do occur naturally. Some bacteria reproduce by cloning themselves, and identical twins share the same genome. Secondly, all humans share 99.9% of the same DNA, therefore are only 0.01% unique. Thirdly, twins can develop differently, due to environmental differences in the womb and after birth. Theoretically, then, cloned humans would also be unique. Lastly, we can assume IVF exists in the world of the novel; therefore, being made in a lab doesn't mean clones are not human. The only real difference, then, between clones and non-clones in the novel is that the former don't have parents and are the property of the government. This suggests society's prejudice is based on false beliefs – much like historical justifications of racism and sexism being based on the myths that people of colour were inferior to white people and women were less intelligent than men because their brains are smaller.

Stem cell research

At the time of the novel's publication, stem cell research was a blooming and controversial field. Scientists extract stem cells from embryos, umbilical cords, amniotic fluid and living tissue to find cures for diseases, regenerate tissue and test new drugs. Some regenerative stem cell therapies already exist (e.g. bone marrow transplants). Researchers have explored the potential for cloning human embryos to extract stem cells, but current practices only extract stem cells from donated IVF embryos or adult tissue.

The novel taps into some of the ethical debates surrounding cloning and stem cell science. Like the cloned animals and embryos used to harvest stem cells, the clones are created for the sole purpose of providing body parts, resulting in physical suffering and early death. The Morningdale scandal discussed in Chapter Twenty-two, in which a scientist named James Morningdale took his research with genetics 'far beyond legal boundaries' (p.258), reflects concerns about the future of biomedicine, ethical subjectivity, and the challenges of preventing injustice and criminal activity.

Genetic engineering and eugenics

The Morningdale scandal also reflects fears held by many that future developments in biomedicine will create a new form of eugenics through scientific genetic engineering. **Eugenics** is the practice of enhancing the gene pool of a population, which dates back to ancient Greece when Plato advocated for marriage and procreation laws to preserve the purity of noble classes. In the late nineteenth century, some Western scientists promoted selective breeding to enhance the quality of populations. This inspired policies and practices in the West (including Britain, America, Australia and many European nations) which included banning interracial marriages and enforcing sterilisation of people who had mental illnesses, disabilities or criminal convictions. Nazi Germany's use of execution and mass sterilisation to 'cleanse' society of Jewish people, dissidents, people with disabilities, and LGBTQI+ people turned many countries against eugenics. However, developments in genetic engineering research in the 1990s ignited fears about a new era of eugenics.

Genetic engineering is the artificial modification of an organism's genes. It is widely used to create genetically modified plants and micro-organisms in agriculture and in human medicine through **gene therapy**. The science used by James Morningdale in the novel (p.258) is presumably **germline engineering**, which involves modifying reproductive cells before fertilisation to change heritable traits. Due to ethical concerns, germline engineering is outlawed in most countries.

Perspectives of the 'human'

The novel poses complex questions about what it means to be human, the value of life and the social implications of scientific progress. Examining how the novel's ideas fit into the spectrum of historical and contemporary perspectives about humans will inform your reading.

Human creation

Western and non-Western cultures have traditionally held different beliefs about life, death and humanity's place in the order of the world. Ancient Judeo-Christian beliefs have had enormous influence on Western thinking, especially in England where Christianity has been prominent since the second century and is the official state religion. Today Christianity is the largest global religion, encompassing one-third of the world's population and reaching across the entire globe. Many dominant beliefs about human existence have roots in the Adam and Eve creation myth and these underpin the debates about clones' humanity in the novel. This story proclaims that God created the universe, made humans in His own image and gave them dominion over animals, and that humanity's duty is to procreate and populate the Earth. Early Christians adopted ancient Greek ideas about human souls, with ideas about the soul's immortality developing in the Middle Ages. In the novel, society's debate over clones' souls is rooted in the Christian belief that every human has a unique soul, created by God and placed into the body at conception.

Another significant Western idea is '**the great chain of being**', dating back to ancient Greece. The theory placed all life and matter on a hierarchy from purely spiritual (thus most eminent and intelligent) to purely material (least eminent and intelligent), with God at the top, followed by angels, humans, animals, plants and minerals. The idea shaped many institutions and ideologies after it was adopted by Christian theology in the Middle Ages and has often been used to justify prejudice.

In the mid-nineteenth century, Charles Darwin's **theory of evolution** revolutionised understanding of the natural world. Nonetheless, many of the assumptions and values of earlier theories survive today in Christianity: structures of inequality, prejudice, and attitudes to the environment. Evidence of this appears in the novel through society's belief in human supremacy, hierarchical values and the perception of clones as being non-human.

Humanism

A major influence on contemporary Western society is **humanism**, a philosophy emphasising the welfare, dignity and autonomy of humans. Originating in the thirteenth century, humanism was a reaction against Christian dogma, arguing that knowledge was achieved through rational thought (rather than divine revelation) and human destiny was the result of human action (rather than God's will). In the eighteenth and nineteenth centuries, humanism underpinned many Enlightenment ideals and led to the decreasing power of monarchies and the Catholic Church in favour of constitutional governments. Humanist ideals are entrenched in structures and systems of all Western societies to this day: values include the dignity of life, human rights, individualism, freedom, self-improvement, progress, secularism and logical reasoning.

Posthumanism

Science fiction writers have long expressed fears about humans playing god by creating sentient machines, mutants or new life forms that threaten humans and society. In the past few decades, developments in biotechnology, cybernetics, artificial intelligence and engineering have made these possibilities less of a fantasy. Opponents of pursuing such advancements warn against egotism and vanity in the quest for perfection, the violation of nature and human dignity, unforeseeable catastrophes and new forms of eugenics.

Since the 1990s, **posthumanism** has gained momentum as a philosophy that welcomes the enhancement of human potential through science and technology. Posthumanists reject the humanist view of people as autonomous agents at the top of a natural hierarchy, arguing we are dependent on and part of an evolving ecosystem. They argue people have always attempted to improve health, life expectancy, athleticism and productivity through technology and science, and therefore genetically and technologically enhanced human beings and artificial life are the next stage of evolution.

GENRE, STRUCTURE & LANGUAGE

Genre

Never Let Me Go is a work of literary fiction which blends and subverts several genres. Typical of a **bildungsroman**, Kathy's story spans childhood to adulthood, focusing on identity formation, maturation and loss of innocence. Breaking convention, Kathy's story doesn't end happily with her finding her true identity or place in society. Likewise, the traditional structure is somewhat inverted as the tragic loss which triggers Kathy's search for meaning occurs at the end of her character arc, rather than the start. Drawing on **romance** and **young adult** tropes, the novel presents Tommy initially as an apparent archetypal love interest for Kathy, making his relationship with Ruth seem illogical and amplifying the tragedy of Tommy and Kathy's limited time together at the end.

As **speculative** fiction (a broad genre featuring non-realistic elements), the novel creates **defamiliarization** by setting events in a recent history that feels authentic, with the exception of the futuristic clones. The schism between past and future, and what's familiar versus what's strange, encourages us to see our world in a new way. Futuristic science, ethical questions and challenging the status quo are typical of **science fiction**; however, the scant use of scientific concepts and details in the novel is atypical of that genre.

Dystopian fiction is a subgenre of science fiction, typically presenting a futuristic world in which an oppressive authority controls citizens through propaganda, surveillance, suppression of free speech, violence and intimidation. Often the society presents a utopian illusion and typically the protagonist questions the system and attempts to fight back. *Never Let Me Go* uses many of these elements; however, Kathy isn't a dissident hero, only clones are oppressed and the novel lacks the genre's usual dark and menacing atmosphere.

The novel also functions as an **allegory** in which the story's world, plot and characters can be interpreted symbolically. Read this way, the clones might symbolise marginalised groups, victims of oppression or exploitation, or all of humanity.

Setting

The novel's present is the late 1990s; however, futuristic clones, nostalgia and lack of historical markers create a timelessness that makes this world seem both real and unreal. The three parts of the novel represent three phases of Kathy's life, each set in a different primary location with physical and symbolic qualities of space and place representing different forms of alienation. As she moves from Hailsham to the Cottages to a bedsit, the size of her home and the number of people she cohabitates with decrease, while conversely her mobility within society increases. Kathy has the most physical freedom when driving around the country as a carer. Yet, at this time she is the most alone and alienated she's ever been. Her reunion with Ruth and Tommy is only possible because she has the unusual privilege of choosing her donors. For most carers, friendships are permanently severed and dislocated all over the country, much like their body parts will be.

Hailsham

Hailsham looks like a traditional English boarding school. Rurality and open fields create an illusion of freedom, while twisting paths, ivy-covered arches and the duck pond evoke wholesome charm. Guardians live in a converted orangery (large conservatories built by the wealthy, from the eighteenth century, to protect exotic plants from the cold), implying the house is a grand historical mansion. However, other details connote confinement and control. The school sits in a valley, obscuring the landscape beyond from view, hinting at the notion of being hidden and buried. Numerous windows make students feel they're being constantly watched and privacy is impossible inside the noisy, crowded house. Fences enclose the property but they don't appear to be in the foreground. The most effective barricade is students' fear of the woods, fuelled by legends about murderers and ghosts. The school's precise location is never stated and, as an adult, Kathy doesn't find it again, which accentuates the impression of Hailsham as an illusion, dislocated from English society.

The Cottages

The Cottages are on an old rundown farm, distinctly less grand and comfortable than Hailsham. There are no fences, so students can come and go. Free from guardians, students enjoy a brief period of 'easy-going days' where time is 'languid' and 'drifting' (p.117).

Recovery centres

The conditions of recovery centres vary markedly. Ruth's centre in Dover is clean, spacious and modern, while Tommy's in Kingsfield is a converted holiday camp with inadequate facilities. (English holiday camps were marketed towards families who couldn't afford more luxurious kinds of holidays, suggesting Tommy's accommodation was quite basic and utilitarian.) This contrast undermines the perception of Hailsham students as privileged, as it seems their allocation to centres is random.

Norfolk

Norfolk is both a real English county and an imagined place symbolising hope, loss and the conflict between fantasy and reality. Featured in each part of the novel, Norfolk also symbolises growing up. As children, students have a notion of Norfolk as being a magical place where the things they lose reappear; it represents the loss of innocence through the teens' disappointing search for Ruth's possible; and when Kathy returns at the end of the novel, it represents letting go of the past.

Structure

Focalisation

The novel is written from Kathy's perspective using **retrospective narration**. Incidences of **direct address** to the reader suggest the narrative is a written account for other clones, stressing Kathy's desire to preserve her memories. The absence of attempts to explain clones' context for a non-clone reader amplifies Kathy's alienation from English society. Positioning the actual readers to view the world through this perspective normalises her reality. Readers have no concrete information about society until Kathy receives it herself, allowing us to feel the destabilising impact of Miss Emily's revelations in Chapter Twenty-two. The reading experience mirrors the clones' stymied process of understanding their existence. Kathy is an **unreliable narrator**: her memories aren't always reliable and her perspective is skewed by indoctrination. Kathy's honesty allows us to trust her, but when we compare our own experience and knowledge to hers we can recognise gaps and obscurities in her perception.

Temporal structure

The novel is organised into three chronological sections. However, the narration is nonlinear, conveying Kathy's thoughts in the present as she recalls her past. In Part One especially, the narration moves back and forth in time in a pattern of interrupted thoughts and tangents, emphasising the fragmented quality of childhood memories.

Motifs

The motif of **copies** and **copying** develops ideas about identity and authenticity. Society views clones as inferior because they are genetic copies; the residents of the Cottages copy behaviours from TV and older students; and Kathy finds a copy of her Judy Bridgewater music cassette in Norfolk. Kathy refers to **driving** frequently, which is a symbol of freedom. A pattern of **losing and finding** is developed through having art taken away by Madame, the Judy Bridgewater tape, Norfolk, Kathy losing Tommy and Ruth after leaving the Cottages, and finding them again only to lose them forever when they die. This ties with the idea of **holding on** to people, memories, the past and hope. Examples include the novel's title, the Judy Bridgewater song of the same name, and Tommy's mental image of a couple in a river.

Style and language

Narrative voice

The use of **first-person point of view** creates an intimacy between readers and Kathy, promoting empathy and identification. The overarching tone of the novel is nostalgic and melancholic, although Kathy's narrative voice is constructed through a prosaic style and predominantly neutral tone. This evokes an ordinariness that belies the sinister circumstances of clones' lives. As a character, Kathy experiences a range of emotions but this is mostly implied through action and figurative devices. When the narration does directly state Kathy's emotion, it's through matter-of-fact reportage of what she felt in the past. In the present, even as she ponders and reflects, the affective texture of the narration is restrained and static. This is incongruous with the fluctuations of narrative tension, which are often jarring for the reader, positioning us to feel horrified not only by the cruelties inflicted on the clones but also by Kathy's perception of them.

Names

The students only have a first name and an initial, underlining their restricted identities and absence of family. **Hailsham** is a compound of *hail*, which is to praise enthusiastically, and *sham*, which means fraudulent and fake. **Guardian** has multiple meanings: protector; guard; parental figure. The guardians fulfil all these roles but, ironically, what they're really protecting is the system that hurts clones. Individually, guardians are referred to by their formal **title** and informal first name, connoting a paradox of detachment and familiarity.

Euphemisms

Euphemisms are used as propaganda, not just to tone down unpleasantness but also to distort meaning and attribute virtuous ideals to horrific things. **Special** is a euphemism for having a specific function (growing organs) but deceptively implies that students are exceptional and valued. The word 'clone' only appears twice in the novel (p.164, p.256), with clone children referred to as **students**, and the process of being cloned as being **copied**. The words **donor**, **donation** and **completing** conceal the brutality of organ harvesting and death, while falsely implying altruism and self-fulfilment. Even calling the main building, Hailsham House (p.49), a **house** is deceptive, providing an illusion of homeliness while concealing the fact that it's an institution of captivity and indoctrination.

Symbolism

Collections are symbols of students' identity. **Art** embodies contradictions as it's used to indoctrinate the children but still provides pleasure. Tommy's animal drawings are a symbol of his ability to thrive, once free of the constraints of Hailsham. Madame's **Gallery** is an illusion: students' work was exhibited to celebrate the school's benefactors rather than the students**. Water** represents forces of time and currents of life, appearing in Kathy's talk with Tommy by the pond, their trips to seaside towns in search of a deferral and Ruth's possible, and Tommy's mental image of a couple in a river. The **boat** in the marshes symbolises clones' lives: being stranded and stuck, mortality, and the beauty in discarded things. References to **trash** and **rubbish** symbolise society's attitudes to clones as worthless and disposable. Society's attitudes are also symbolised through Madame fearing clones as though they're **spiders**, implying clones are creepy and dangerous. Miss Emily's **bedside cabinet** is an object she's had since Hailsham: selling it symbolises Hailsham closing and the failure of her project. Her desire to protect it to ensure she gets a 'fair price' (p.252) mirrors her caring for the clones to ensure their body parts maintain maximum commodified value.

CHAPTER-BY-CHAPTER ANALYSIS

Part One

Chapter One (pp.3–12)

Summary: *Kathy reflects on her career as a carer and recalls Tommy being mocked at Hailsham.*

Kathy's introduction in the opening sentences seems perfunctory but these details develop significance as the novel progresses – thirty-one is old for a clone and her lengthy time as a carer is unusual. References to donors and carers allude to organ harvesting, but the full context is not yet clear. Reflecting on her choice to become Ruth's carer suggests Kathy and Ruth's relationship will be significant, while her recollection of conversations with a donor reveals Hailsham students' privilege.

We're introduced to twelve-year-old Kathy and her friends at Hailsham. Her recollection of Tommy being bullied establishes his outsider status. Stepping away from her friends to approach Tommy shows she has the capacity to go against the crowd. The tone of the narration and the pastoral imagery conceal the brutal truth of clones' lives, positioning readers to presume these students' childhoods are somewhat normal.

Q What are the clues to past tensions between Ruth and Kathy?

Q Kathy is an unreliable narrator. Find quotes that indicate subjectivity and flaws in her perspective.

Chapter Two (pp.13–24)

Summary: *Kathy recalls the extent of Tommy's exclusion and when things started to change for him.*

Artistic pursuits are highly valued at Hailsham, with the students' creations forming cultural capital that gives their lives purpose and influences how others perceive them. Exchanges are significant events, with the dual purpose of allowing students to acquire personal possessions and reinforcing the value of producing creative works. Tommy's ostracism indicates that these values and practices generate inequality. The guardians' power is conveyed through Miss Geraldine's role in alienating Tommy, and Miss Lucy's talk affecting Tommy's confidence.

Q How do Kathy and Ruth's adult recollections of Exchanges imply deception at Hailsham?

Chapter Three (pp.25–36)

Summary: *Kathy recounts meeting Tommy by the pond and recalls an earlier time when she learnt of Madame's fear of the students.*

This chapter conveys the rigidity and restraint of life at Hailsham. Students have limited knowledge of or access to the outside world, they lack privacy and obediently abide by strict rules prescribed both by the guardians and themselves. Secrecy around Madame and the Gallery heightens the insinuation that students are kept in the dark about the truth of their existence. Tommy's revelation about Miss Lucy's anger piques Kathy's long-held suspicions that things aren't quite as they seem. She recalls an earlier incident when, aged eight, she and her friends set about testing a theory that Madame might be scared of the students. The incident not only confirms their suspicions but is profoundly upsetting.

Key point

The scene with Madame is the first indication that society doesn't see the clones in the way that Hailsham has implied. Being viewed as a creepy-crawly connotes objectification and dehumanisation. The mirror simile conveys how this moment disrupted Kathy's self-image and will have a lasting impact on her identity.

Q What kinds of things are the students naive and ill-informed about?

Chapter Four (pp.37–48)

Summary: *Kathy reflects on the tokens controversy, the Sales and first meeting Ruth.*

Kathy reveals that her need to make sense of her memories was triggered by the impending end of her time as a carer, hinting at the importance of this milestone and highlighting the significance of childhood experiences in shaping identity. This chapter establishes the importance of Tommy and Ruth in Kathy's story. Contradictions and irony throughout the chapter emphasise the artificiality of Hailsham. Having work taken away by Madame is perceived as a great honour, which is contradicted by the commodification of students' art as currency for Exchanges. Students' collections provide a sense of individuality, which seems disingenuous given the triviality of the items and the inevitable disappointment of the Sales. These customs appear to be shallow attempts to give the students a false sense of agency.

Q What is the cause of the increasing silence regarding Madame?

Chapter Five (pp.49–60)

Summary: *Kathy recalls Ruth's secret guard game and Ruth's lie that Miss Geraldine gifted her a pencil case.*

The 'secret guard' game – to thwart a supposed plot to kidnap Miss Geraldine – was probably invented and definitely led by Ruth, revealing more of her controlling tendencies. The fervour with which the other girls play along reflects a desire to please Ruth. Playing make-believe is a normal childhood pastime, reminding us that the students are innocent children. Their fixation on the abduction plot and the ominousness of the woods highlights fear and ignorance about the outside world.

Kathy's uncertainty about the reason for her hostility to Moira illustrates the confusion that came with growing up at Hailsham. Parallels between the secret guard game and Ruth's lie about the pencil case establish a pattern in Ruth's personality while also revealing a change in Kathy's tolerance of Ruth's dishonesty as they grow older. Plotting to catch Ruth in her lie gives Kathy a sense of power, which dissipates the second Ruth gets upset, emphasising the power of Kathy's loyalty to Ruth. This scene hints at the fragility beneath Ruth's tough exterior.

Q What are the common threads between the chess anecdote and other memories in this chapter?

Chapter Six (pp.61–75)

Summary: *Kathy remembers her efforts to make amends for hurting Ruth, her Judy Bridgewater tape and a confusing incident with a tearful Madame.*

This chapter includes the first reference to the song 'Never Let Me Go' and the novel's title (p.69). Kathy's interpretation of the song, which she acknowledges is wrong, and Madame's tears at the sight of Kathy pretending to hold a baby express the cruelty of clones' infertility. Madame's reaction is confusing to Kathy, both as a child and an adult, enhancing Madame's mysterious and sinister nature. Kathy's memories move back and forth through time to show how the students were taught about the donor system in a piecemeal manner that sugar-coated the truth.

Kathy and Ruth's relationship is developed through mutual efforts to please each other and their reluctance to speak honestly about their feelings. The girls' literal perception of Norfolk as a 'lost corner' (p.65) signifies the black-and-white perspective of childhood and emphasises their ignorance about the world. Miss Lucy's smoking dialogue alludes to the students' purpose as donors and the fact that their bodies do not belong to them.

Q Which details in this chapter convey the culture and norms of life at Hailsham? How does growing up in this environment shape the students and their perspectives?

Chapter Seven (pp.76–87)

Summary: *Kathy reflects on Miss Lucy's speech about donations and the students' evolving attitudes to their future.*

Kathy's memories of Hailsham fall into two eras, which alludes to a loss of innocence as she entered adolescence. Miss Lucy's speech, Kathy's discussion with Tommy and Kathy's narration illuminate Hailsham's indoctrination methods. Making jokes about sex and donations is, in part, indicative of typical adolescent naivety but in the context of the donor program, the 'unzipping' jokes emphasise students' ignorance (p.87). Kathy recalls a conversation with Tommy, long after leaving Hailsham, in which he questioned the students' disregard for Miss Lucy. As he says they were 'selfish', and 'old enough' to consider others' feelings (p.87), it seems they were taught not to think about the guardians as individuals, to maintain a disconnection from them.

Q How does Kathy's perspective and retrospection in the final paragraph of the chapter help to develop themes?

Chapter Eight (pp.88–97)

Summary: *At sixteen, Kathy's life becomes more confusing after an unsettling encounter with Miss Lucy and as teens develop sexual urges.*

Miss Lucy's demeanour in Room 22 suggests she's struggling with her job. Kathy's discomfort indicates that Miss Lucy's vulnerability unsettles her sense of Hailsham as a safe place. Kathy and her peers face typical adolescent experiences as they become interested in relationships and sex, and develop anxieties about their identity. Their isolation, limited access to books and lack of guidance imply deliberate censorship which results in confusion. The sudden revelation of Tommy and Ruth's relationship, introduced at a point when they are in conflict, is jarring and subverts the archetypal coming-of-age love story. This twist emphasises Ruth's overbearing influence on Kathy's life and the notion that growing up in Hailsham has thwarted Kathy's development.

Q In what ways does adult Kathy have more insight than her younger self?

Q Why does Kathy feel isolated from her peers?

Chapter Nine (pp.98–109)

Summary: *Kathy recalls Ruth employing her help to reunite with Tommy; Miss Lucy leaves Hailsham.*

Cynthia's comment about Kathy being Ruth's 'natural successor' as Tommy's girlfriend suggests Kathy is considered Ruth's inferior (p.98). It also indicates that other students expect Kathy and Tommy to get together, reinforcing earlier implications about the potential for romance between the pair. Kathy's eagerness to accept Cynthia's theory, swiftly abandoning her plot to have sex with Harry, suggests that she does have feelings for Tommy. However, she is easily persuaded to help Ruth reunite with Tommy, reinforcing Kathy's loyalty to Ruth. Miss Lucy's change of opinion about Tommy's art, together with Kathy's narration linking back to the scene in Room 22, are hints that significant conflicts are brewing between Miss Lucy and the other guardians. Kathy and Tommy's confusion about this underlines the disconnect between guardians and students.

Q Why do you think Tommy has a change of heart about reconciling with Ruth after learning of Miss Lucy's departure?

Part Two

Chapter Ten (pp.113–23)

Summary: *Kathy recalls the early days at the Cottages.*

This chapter moves the narrative forward to the era in which Kathy and her friends first experience the world outside Hailsham. For the most part, Kathy fondly remembers this as a time of intimacy and peacefulness. However, as an adult she recognises that the image of huddling with her friends on the first day embodies their enduring fear and alienation. Describing them as being unable 'to let each other go' alludes to the title (p.118). The essays reflect students' desire to hold on to the security and familiarity of Hailsham. Keffers' disdain for the students hints at how society views them. Their modelling of behaviours from television reflects the students' desire to be part of a society from which they are excluded and which they do not understand. This contradiction underpins the insecurities and anxiety that fuels the conflict between Ruth and Kathy.

Q How do descriptive details on page 117 evoke a particular mood in conveying life at the Cottages? How does this contribute to themes?

Chapter Eleven (pp.124–35)

Summary: *Kathy reflects on conflicts with Ruth, attitudes to students who'd left the Cottages and Tommy finding her in the boiler hut with Steve's porn magazines.*

Kathy's reflections on betrayal offer a deeper understanding of the contradictions in her relationship with Ruth and how moving to the Cottages created new tensions as they struggled with anxieties about fitting in and growing up. Kathy's confession about sexual urges reminds us how young and vulnerable the students are, despite their determination to think and behave maturely. It also highlights their isolation by emphasising the absence of parental guidance. Kathy and Ruth's attitudes to their collections represent contrasting perspectives on adjusting to their new life. The Hailsham culture of secrecy and reticence persists at the Cottages, with avoidance of discussing the future. Kathy feels safe with Tommy, unashamed when he finds her with the porn magazines, demonstrating their sincere and intimate bond.

Q How do you think the students' infertility and living arrangements affect their attitudes to sex?

Chapter Twelve (pp.136–43)

Summary: *Kathy recalls the theory of possibles and Ruth's dream future.*

Incongruities throughout the chapter emphasise flaws in the clones' perceptions, positioning readers to question the principles underpinning the donor program. Kathy's scepticism about Chrissie and Rodney contrasts with the cosy intimacy of life at the Cottages; fantasising about mundane professions contradicts the idealism of 'dream futures' (p.140); and the desire for an autonomous life conflicts with the reality of donations. The theories about possibles appear naive; however, the 'awkwardness' surrounding the topic suggests a deeper awareness of the dark reality (p.137). Structurally, the chapter begins and ends with reference to the Norfolk trip, indicating the event's importance.

Q How does this chapter foreground ideas related to the trip to Norfolk?

Q What is the symbolic function of the magazine on page 142?

Chapter Thirteen (pp.144–53)

Summary: *Kathy recounts the trip to Norfolk and the discussion of deferrals.*

Glimpses into Ruth's anxiety convey her fragility. Kathy is sympathetic and forgiving, both in the moment and as narrator. Nonetheless, Ruth's actions and dialogue reinforce her manipulative qualities as she fawns over the veterans. In Norfolk, Rodney and Chrissie speak freely about topics considered taboo at the Cottages, demonstrating the restrictive environment the students live in, despite the appearance of freedom. The topic of deferrals is another example of the myth-like rumours that circulate in the absence of reliable information. This rumour emphasises the superior status of Hailsham students among the clone community, while the belief that true love might be the key to freedom characterises the clones as childlike innocents clinging to hopeful fantasies.

Q Why do you think Chrissie and Rodney care about deferrals even though they believe the option is only available to Hailsham students?

Chapter Fourteen (pp.154–65)

Summary: *In Norfolk, tensions build between the students when they find Ruth's suspected possible.*

Talk of deferrals and Ruth's nastiness towards Tommy in the previous chapter has soured the atmosphere among the group. Ruth's moods, whims and actions dominate the group, with others frequently attempting to placate her. While Kathy feels able to read Ruth's feelings (for example, she states 'I could tell Ruth was furious', p.154), she's less sure of how to read Rodney and Chrissie. This emphasises the bond between Kathy and Ruth from having grown up together. Disappointment about Ruth's possible causes friction which culminates in Ruth's angry outburst. She overtly refers to the students as 'clones' who have been modelled from 'trash' (p.164). This blatant defiance of the culture of restrained politeness speaks to the students' deep-seated fears about who they are and how the world perceives them. Settings function symbolically throughout the chapter, with the open-plan office representing a world the clones will never be part of and the studio being a typical gallery, which is distinctly unlike the Exchanges at Hailsham and Madame's Gallery.

Q Which details imply the veterans resent Hailsham students?

Chapter Fifteen (pp.166–81)

Summary: *In Norfolk, Tommy and Kathy search for the Judy Bridgewater cassette and speak freely about deferrals, the Gallery and sex.*

Tommy's desire to find the Judy Bridgewater cassette conveys his affection for Kathy. Away from Ruth and the veterans, Tommy and Kathy are happy and relaxed. Tommy's theories about Madame's Gallery and deferrals represent the students' desire for autonomy. Tommy reassuring Kathy that her sexual urges are normal, which contradict Ruth's comments in Chapter Eleven, further conveys the dysfunction in Kathy and Ruth's friendship. This is amplified by Ruth's overt friendliness at the end of the chapter while she is also refusing to admit wrongdoing or apologise.

Q Why do you think Kathy got tearful while discussing sex?

Q Why do you think Kathy didn't tell Ruth about the cassette?

Chapter Sixteen (pp.182–93)

Summary: *Kathy reflects on Tommy's drawings, and Ruth's trick to undermine Tommy and Kathy's friendship.*

The Norfolk trip is a turning point for the characters; however, their sustained avoidance of discussing difficult subjects persists as time passes and more students leave the Cottages. Tommy shows Kathy his drawings, which she recognises as original and skilful. Kathy feels she is losing her connection to Hailsham and is angered by Ruth's pretence that she has forgotten details of their past. Ruth sees the Judy Bridgewater cassette and, while she appears nonchalant, her jealousy is revealed when the three friends meet in the churchyard after Ruth coaxes Kathy into laughing about Tommy's drawings and his theory about the Gallery, and twists Kathy's words to cause a rift between her and Tommy. Kathy's narration contains numerous doubts, regrets and reflections that convey her shock at Ruth's brazen duplicity, the difficulty of the situation and Kathy's conflicting feelings for Ruth and Tommy.

Q How has Tommy changed from who he was at Hailsham?

Chapter Seventeen (pp.194–9)

Summary: *Kathy recalls her final days at the Cottages.*

The churchyard incident causes an irreparable rift between the trio. Kathy's narration implies they were naive about the significance of their falling out. Her regret that they hadn't 'kept a tighter hold of one another' refers to the title (p.194), reinforcing the importance of the trio's relationship and foregrounding the significance of their future reunion. Once again, Ruth uses Kathy's sexual relationships to undermine her bond with Tommy, suggesting Ruth is threatened by Tommy and Kathy's connection. Ruth's pretence about forgetting details from Hailsham seems like a deliberate attempt to push Kathy away. Deciding to leave the Cottages marks a turning point for Kathy. She no longer feels tied to Hailsham or her friendships and willingly enters the next phase of her life.

Q Which details in this chapter convey ideas about loss?

Part Three

Chapter Eighteen (pp.203–13)

Summary: *Kathy reflects on meeting Laura and becoming Ruth's carer.*

This chapter marks the shift into the third part of the novel, which focuses on Kathy's adulthood. Comparing herself to those who struggle with caring, Kathy conveys how her adaptability allows her to cope with a life of solitude and servitude. The chance meeting with Laura highlights the adverse conditions carers contend with. Laura's sluggish and demoralised affect is a stark contrast to her previously lively and playful personality. Kathy's memory of the clown's balloons, held together by string, and her imagining them being cut loose, functions as a metaphor for her feelings of disconnection now that Hailsham has closed. The decision to become Ruth's carer marks a desire to resolve the past. The pair's refusal to address unresolved conflicts creates distrust and apprehension. Ruth's desire to see the boat signifies a need to escape the brutality and mundanity of her life as well as a desire to reunite Kathy with Tommy.

Q How does this chapter convey a change in Ruth's character and how might this relate to the novel's themes?

Chapter Nineteen (pp.214–32)

Summary: *Kathy recalls the trip to see the beached boat; Ruth apologises to Tommy and Kathy and encourages them to seek a deferral.*

The trip to the boat echoes the trio's earlier trip to Norfolk, with several details in the dialogue drawing clear parallels and differences, emphasising the loss and suffering characters have experienced in the time that has passed. Ruth has changed considerably. She's calmer, more honest and her apologies suggest she has been humbled by being so close to death. However, her reluctance to admit remembering her youthful fantasies is reminiscent of the old Ruth and implies she is still insecure. Being a carer and in good health makes Kathy the leader of the group, yet deeply entrenched beliefs about the superiority of donors are evident in Tommy and Ruth's dialogue. Ruth's insistence that Tommy and Kathy should seek a deferral is an attempt to make amends and implies that, even as adults, the clones have a distorted view of reality. The fantasy of deferrals contradicts the characters' pride in being donors, indicating that, deep down, they still wish their lives to mean more. Ruth's death at the end of the chapter is another major turning point. Being Ruth's carer has allowed the pair to make peace, and Ruth's death frees Kathy from loyalty to Ruth, so she can be with Tommy.

Q Why do you think Tommy doesn't react to Ruth's admission to cheating on him?

Chapter Twenty (pp.233–40)

Summary: *Kathy becomes Tommy's carer; they plan to visit Madame.*

The naturalness with which Kathy and Tommy begin their romance is juxtaposed with the sombre mood evoked by Tommy's ill health. The awkwardness around deferrals suggests they know their plan is childish and unrealistic. Kathy's sense that Tommy's drawings have become stale emphasises their desperation and the futility of their desire to stall time. Kathy keeps her doubts to herself and pursues their plan enthusiastically, her unsettled feelings signalling an inner conflict between her love for Tommy and her fear of the inevitability of losing him.

Q What types of experiences provide happiness for Tommy and Kathy? How does this represent their relationship, goals and values?

Chapter Twenty-one (pp.241–50)

Summary: *Kathy and Tommy visit Madame.*

Kathy's anxiety prior to visiting Madame, and the details of everything that went wrong that day, create a foreboding mood. Following Madame along the streets reminds Kathy of the trip to find Ruth's possible, implying naive foolishness in their plan and foreshadowing their disappointment. Madame's house, behaviour and dialogue are depicted with theatricality and mystery. She appears always to be one step ahead and is condescending as she entertains Tommy and Kathy's story, all along knowing truths they do not. This reinforces her power, while her haughtiness exemplifies her feelings about clones. The sudden reveal of Miss Emily, who was never expected to be there and who now seems to have been Madame's superior at Hailsham, despite the students always believing the reverse, is symbolic of the impending revelations that will reframe Tommy and Kathy's understanding of their existence.

Key point

Madame and Miss Emily symbolise the social structures underpinning the donor system. Miss Emily emerging from the shadows exemplifies how the truth has always been just out of reach for the clones. Her 'frail and contorted' appearance (p.250) contrasts with Madame's unchanged and stoic presentation, representing the system as having a facade of authority and righteousness that conceals the ugly truth of its inhumanity and the crumbling of its hubristic ideals.

Q How do specific details on pages 249–50 reflect Miss Emily and Madame's relationship and their roles in the donor program?

Chapter Twenty-two (pp.251–70)

Summary: *Miss Emily reveals the truth about Hailsham.*

This chapter is the climax of the novel, as Kathy and Tommy learn the truth and have their hopes crushed. This is the only time we get insight into Miss Emily and Madame's perspectives on how the donor system functions. The revelations disrupt the previous representations of Hailsham and its students. Reframing the purpose of students' art as proving clones 'had souls at all' (p.255), Madame's interpretation of Kathy's dance and Miss Emily's ambivalence underline the deception which has shaped how Kathy and Tommy have understood the world.

Irony and incongruities emphasise the hypocrisy and cruelty of society. Miss Emily claims their movement wanted to treat clones humanely. However, Madame still calls them 'creatures' (p.267) and Miss Emily admits her repulsion, showing more concern for her bedside cabinet than for Kathy and Tommy. Kathy's narration is flat and unemotional, jarring with the heightened tension of the couple's hopes being crushed and their world being flipped upside down.

Tommy's emotional explosion in the field mirrors his tantrum in Chapter One, giving weight to Kathy's suggestion that he always knew something was wrong. Kathy and Tommy holding on to each other links to the title and the recurring motif of holding on and letting go.

Key point

Miss Emily and Madame are constructed as elitist and prejudiced. They perceive clones as inferior beings in need of their protection, which is at odds with their claims of altruism. Their hierarchical values are shown through Miss Emily's employment of George, whom she refers to as 'the big Nigerian man' (p.251), which has echoes of the history of indentured servitude in Britain. Likewise, her assumptions about the ineptitude of the removalists signify class discrimination.

Q For all their dedication to their project, Miss Emily and Madame seem wilfully resigned to their inability to change anything. Do you think this is a fair position or an avoidance of responsibility?

Chapter Twenty-three (pp.271–82)

Summary: *Kathy and Tommy's relationship comes to an end.*

Knowing their lives have been based on lies, Kathy and Tommy are now defined more by their present roles than by their shared history. Tommy's impending death and their loss of hope cause resentment to hang over them, as though the other's presence reminds them of their loss and shame. Tommy's fears about his fourth donation from stories of donors retaining consciousness after dying emphasise the cruelty of the system. The image of still-conscious bodies stuck in an endless cycle of being cut up and defiled reinforces the brutality of organ harvesting and the injustice of donors' bodies not belonging to them. Tommy's image of two people struggling to hold on to each other in a river symbolises their relationship at this point in their lives and alludes to the title. The end of their relationship marks an acceptance of their fate.

Key point

The resolution ties up the themes of the novel and provides closure to Kathy's story. After Tommy dies, Kathy accepts she cannot return to the past. Holding on to her memories is the only thing she can control and doing so brings her comfort and peace. She visits Norfolk in remembrance of Tommy. The image of the fence alludes to all the barriers and restraints in the clones' lives. Kathy imagines all the rubbish and debris along the fence as lost things which have blown in on the wind, subverting Ruth's previous comments about clones being trash and alluding to their childhood idea of Norfolk. Imagining Tommy in the field indicates a final goodbye and confirms he is still alive in her memories.

Q What secret does Tommy reveal to Kathy and why do you think he reveals it now?

Q What is the mood of the resolution and how does this contribute to the themes?

CHARACTERS & RELATIONSHIPS

Kathy

Key quotes

'But I didn't say or do anything. It was partly, I suppose, that I was so floored by the fact that Ruth would come out with such a trick. I remember a huge tiredness coming over me, a kind of lethargy in the face of the tangled mess before me.' (p.193)

'I kept seeing those balloons again. I thought about Hailsham closing, and how it was like someone coming along with a pair of shears and snipping the balloon strings just where they entwined above the man's fist. Once that happened, there'd be no real sense in which those balloons belonged with each other any more.' (p.209)

Kathy is a rounded character with a fully realised and nuanced personality. Part of what makes her so human is her many contradictions: she's stoic but empathetic; self-conscious but decisive; and while she can be observant and analytical, she is also naive and resigned to her fate. As a dynamic character she undergoes a psychological transformation, learning how to find fulfilment in her life despite having little freedom and few choices.

The opening paragraphs establish a conflict between Kathy's pride in her accomplishments as a carer and a desire to assure her reader of her humility. This self-consciousness is a trait we come to see she has had since childhood. She's easily embarrassed in situations that draw attention to her or to the shame of being a clone. Fear of judgement makes her guarded, which we see when she hides from her friends her distress about losing her Judy Bridgewater tape and in her reluctance to express her feelings with Ruth. She relishes moments of privacy, suggesting that living in the hectic environment of a crowded institution is overwhelming. At the Cottages, she worries her sexual urges aren't normal and obediently follows unspoken rules. In adulthood, she's more self-assured and her pride in her work bolsters her self-confidence. Nonetheless she appreciates the solitude of a carer's life. Driving solo around the countryside provides moments of autonomy and frees her from the pressure of others' expectations. Once a defence mechanism, Kathy's stoicism evolves into a pragmatic mindset that eases the emotional and physical burden of caring for dying people.

As a child, Kathy often goes against the crowd and thinks independently. We see this when she breaks away from her friends to comfort Tommy after his outburst on the football field and when she notices 'odd little things' about Miss Lucy that other students miss (p.76). However, these qualities are always in conflict with her fear of confrontation. She keeps most of her questions to herself and gets angry when others broach taboo topics with guardians. She's conciliatory with Ruth, who exploits her loyalty and nonconfrontational personality in particularly cruel ways, although as Kathy grows older she becomes less tolerant of Ruth's manipulation. Her bond with Tommy stems from them 'wondering and asking questions' about themselves together (p.72); however, they never directly question clones' lack of autonomy over their lives or bodies. Seeking a deferral with Tommy reveals a desire for more than her life allows, although, as she believes deferrals exist as part of the system of her world, they wouldn't be breaking any rules by pursuing one. When their hopes are crushed, they accept that their fate is sealed. Even after Miss Emily's revelations about the Hailsham project and society's apathy and cruelty, Kathy doesn't consider her life could or should be any different.

Kathy's relationships with Ruth and Tommy are at the heart of the tragedy and triumph of her story. Despite all her deprivation, Kathy's life is gratifying and meaningful because she has loved and been loved. Recounting her past preserves her memories and allows her to hold on to Tommy and Ruth after they've died. Her narration is nostalgic but not sentimental. Ishiguro's inclusion of the ups and downs, tested loyalties and fights, and Ruth's cruelty and manipulation all characterise Kathy as honest in her retelling of events and convey the idea that meaningful relationships require acceptance and forgiveness. When Kathy leaves the Cottages, it seems her relationships with Tommy and Ruth have run their course, and it's only when Laura encourages Kathy to become Ruth's carer that they reunite. Consequently, Kathy and Ruth resolve their conflicts, and Kathy and Tommy can finally be together. The tragedy is that it all seems too late, and so Kathy must watch the other two suffer through donations, and lose them again when they die.

Kathy's passive acceptance of her destiny can be read in a few ways. One interpretation is that she has internalised society's attitudes. A pivotal event occurs when she's eight and sees herself as a fearful, repulsive thing in Madame's eyes. This 'troubling' notion creates a schism in her identity that stays with her all her life (p.36). Seeing herself perceived as a 'spider' (p.35), belonging in the shadows, reinforces the belief that clones are subordinate. Kathy wouldn't conceive there to be any place for her in broader society and challenging this would only mean having to face society's disgust. Another explanation may be that indoctrinating children distorts their perceptions so severely that it's impossible for them to ever see the truth. Alternatively, it could be argued that Kathy's acceptance isn't passive, that she actively accepts what she can and cannot control, allowing her to make the best of the life she has. In this regard, she wrestles back some power by controlling her outlook and holding on to her dignity.

Key point

Written in the style of an autobiographical testimony, Kathy's narration subverts her society's view that her life and purpose can only be 'completed' through organ donation and death. She reclaims autonomy by choosing to make being a carer her purpose and omitting her time as a donor from her life story. While her prosaic narration can be interpreted as denying or lacking full cognisance of the atrocities inflicted on her, the focus on relationships as what gives life meaning evokes an overarching tone of gratitude. In the end, despite everything she's lost and been denied, a self-determined purpose and authentic human connections have made her life complete.

Ruth

Key quotes

'We're modelled from *trash*. Junkies, prostitutes, winos, tramps. Convicts, maybe, just so long as they aren't psychos. That's what we come from.' (Ruth, p.164)

'It should have been you two. I'm not pretending I didn't always see that. Of course I did, as far back as I can remember. But I kept you apart. I'm not asking you to forgive me for that. That's not what I'm after just now. What I want is for you to put it right.' (Ruth, p.228)

Ruth is Kathy's best friend and the leader of their group at Hailsham. She can be kind and sweet, such as when she gives Kathy a new cassette to replace the lost Judy Bridgewater tape and acts as Kathy's trusted confidant during their night-time talks. However, Ruth can also be bossy, hot-tempered and manipulative, twisting things to get her way and turning on people who challenge her. She often belittles and is cruel to the people who love her most. Eventually, she tricks Kathy into laughing at Tommy's drawings, giving her ammunition to undermine Kathy and Tommy's friendship. This prompts Kathy to leave the Cottages, severing her relationship with them both.

Ruth pretends a lot, concocting fantasies in order to feel important and powerful. Her secret guard game provides a fantasy that she has special favour with Miss Geraldine and is privy to secret knowledge. It also gives Ruth 'enormous authority' which she yields arbitrarily by expelling others and changing theories at whim (p.52). She puts on airs to make herself look superior, such as when she insinuates Miss Geraldine gave her a pencil case and when ingratiating herself with Chrissie and Rodney by encouraging the idea that Hailsham students can receive deferrals.

Much of this behaviour suggests Ruth is deeply insecure. Kathy frequently comments that Ruth takes fantasies and rumours further than others. At the Cottages Ruth is anxious to fit in with the veterans. She tries to prove she's mature by copying the veterans' mannerisms and pretending to forget things about Hailsham. This infuriates Kathy, who feels Ruth is being fake and betraying both Hailsham and Kathy. Ruth's devastation after the disappointment with her possible in Norfolk reveals her fragile sense of self. It's the only time a student uses the word 'clone', and stating that they come from 'trash' and 'the gutter' reveals she's deeply aware of, and hurt by, society's perceptions (p.164).

Ruth is markedly different as an adult. She's still touchy but more subdued and submissive. Admitting to deliberately keeping Tommy and Kathy apart suggests she didn't have real feelings for Tommy and only maintained the relationship out of fear of being left behind. Giving them Madame's address and insisting they seek a deferral reveals the sincerity of her apology and a desire to make amends. Reconciling her past with Kathy is healing for them both and gives Ruth peace as she faces death.

Tommy

Key quotes

'For all their busy, metallic features, there was something sweet, even vulnerable about each of them. I remembered him telling me, in Norfolk, that he worried, even as he created them, how they'd protect themselves or be able to reach and fetch things ...' (p.185)

'I keep thinking about this river somewhere, with the water moving really fast. And these two people in the water, trying to hold onto each other, holding on as hard as they can, but in the end it's just too much. The current's too strong. They've got to let go, drift apart. That's how I think it is with us. It's a shame, Kath, because we've loved each other all our lives. But in the end, we can't stay together forever.' (Tommy, p.277)

In the exposition, Tommy is portrayed as an outsider at Hailsham. Other students consider his lack of artistic ability as a weakness and his lack of effort as proof he's a 'layabout' (p.10). Miss Lucy's assurance that he's special and doesn't need to be creative completely changes Tommy's outlook. He becomes more confident and stops losing his temper, which results in other students giving him less trouble. Kathy is one of the few people who sees past Tommy's differences and they develop a deeply caring and affectionate relationship. While there's always a sense that his feelings for Kathy go beyond friendship, as Ruth's boyfriend he's loving and loyal – perhaps too much so, as he tolerates her belittling and ignoring him.

As the novel develops, it becomes clearer that what really makes Tommy different is that he doesn't see things the way others do. After their visit with Madame and Miss Emily, Kathy wonders if he somehow always knew the truth about Hailsham. From an early age, Tommy is logical and straightforward. He's honest and genuine, never buying into manipulative games or pretence, and doesn't always understand unspoken rules. Pondering the purpose of Madame's Gallery begins in childhood. He suspects there's more to it than they've been told and, as he gets older, develops a theory about deferrals. While it's not true, it is a logical and well-thought-out theory based on the knowledge he has. It fills him with hope, inspiring him to draw again, which he continues for many years, but is also what leads to the crushing realisation that his life has been a lie.

At the Cottages, Tommy can create beautiful art because he's not limited by the constraints of Hailsham. Like Tommy himself, and all clones, his animals are not what they first appear to be. Kathy must look closely to see beyond the 'tiny canals, weaving tendons, miniature screws and wheels' to the unique and complex creatures they are (p.184–5). Their beauty is in their contradictions – they're tiny but immensely detailed, both artificial and alive, metallic but vulnerable. Tommy puts great care into creating them. However, as Tommy and Kathy prepare to visit Madame, his drawings lose their vibrancy and become 'almost like they'd been copied', adding weight to Kathy's worry that they're being foolish to seek a deferral (p.237).

Tommy's relationship with Kathy is central to both characters' transformations. They're initially drawn together by a shared need to understand themselves and Hailsham, and their conversations throughout adolescence provide comfort and reassurance. The Judy

Bridgewater tape and Norfolk are important symbols in their story. Tommy's affection is evident in his desire to find Kathy's lost tape in Norfolk, an idea he holds on to for years and fulfils when they're living at the Cottages. When they finally get together as adults, they fall into a natural and loving rhythm and seeking a deferral represents their desire to hold on to each other. The idea of holding on relates to the title of the novel and of the Judy Bridgewater song, referred to again in the scene of Kathy holding Tommy in the field and Tommy's imagining of a couple in a river. Kathy's return to Norfolk after Tommy's death is like a memorial and she resolves to hold on to him in her memories.

Miss Emily and Madame

Key quotes

'Madame *was* afraid of us. But she was afraid of us in the same way someone might be afraid of spiders. We hadn't been ready for that. It had never occurred to us to wonder how *we* would feel, being seen like that, being the spiders.' (p.35)

'I can see … that it might look as though you were simply pawns in a game. It can certainly be looked at like that. But think of it. You were lucky pawns.' (Miss Emily, p.261)

As head guardian, Miss Emily has a commanding presence that keeps students in line and makes them feel safe. As a child, Kathy notices a few clues that something is not quite right with Miss Emily, such as the loose strands of hair that belie her otherwise ordered appearance and her wandering around talking to herself 'in a dream' (p.43). Nonetheless, Kathy fully trusts and respects Miss Emily, just as all the students do. In contrast, students find Madame creepy and presume she's Miss Emily's superior. Initially, Kathy and her friends interpret Madame's aloofness as 'snooty' until Ruth suggests she's scared of the students (pp.32–3). Considering this a ridiculous prospect, the girls play a prank to test the theory, only to discover Ruth was right and thus experiencing their first real insight into how the world sees them.

When Kathy and Tommy visit Madame, she toys with them before revealing Miss Emily to be her equal and co-founder of Hailsham. Miss Emily is unnervingly cavalier as she shatters every illusion Kathy and Tommy had about Hailsham with her admission of being repulsed by clones and having to 'fight back' her 'dread' every day (p.264). Miss Emily provides direct insight into the society that exists outside of Kathy's perspective, illuminating clones' status as commodified objects. The motives behind Hailsham are revealed but claims of benevolence are undermined by the women's condescending and infantilising dialogue. Madame's repetition of 'poor creatures' (p.267) reinforces that she doesn't see clones as human and Miss Emily seems more concerned about her cabinet than about Tommy and Kathy. While Miss Emily is impassively resigned to her project's failures, Madame is bitter. Both women lack concern for the clones' suffering and expect Tommy and Kathy to be grateful.

As **symbolic characters**, Miss Emily and Madame represent the failures of twentieth-century humanitarian and welfare initiatives that purport to help the less fortunate but in reality do nothing to address issues of autonomy and agency. They are characterised as wealthy philanthropists with self-serving motives. Miss Emily's feeble and decrepit appearance in Part Three symbolises the downfall of Hailsham and the frailty of the women's idealistic rationalisations.

Miss Lucy

Key quote

'The problem, as I see it, is that you've been told and not told. You've been told, but none of you really understand, and I dare say, some people are quite happy to leave it that way. But I'm not. If you're going to have decent lives, then you've got to know and know properly.' (Miss Lucy, pp.79–80)

Miss Lucy struggles with some of the methods at Hailsham, growing increasingly angry about students being lied to. She is a foil to Miss

Emily in that she believes the students have a right to know the truth, while Miss Emily justifies the deception as protecting the students from the 'horrors' of their reality (p.256). Miss Lucy has a profound impact on Tommy when she gives him permission to stop worrying about creating and tells him it's okay to be different. Years later, she changes her tune, telling him art is important 'not just because it's evidence' but also because he'll 'get a lot from it, just for [himself]' (p.106). She admits Madame's Gallery is more important than she had realised, indicating perhaps she recognises that the future of Hailsham relies on ongoing support from investors and politicians, or simply that the students' art may be the only way to change people's views of clones. Whatever her motive though, the impact of her saying this is that Tommy continues to believe that the Gallery has some mysterious importance, which leads to his theory about deferrals and the visit to Madame's house that ends in heartbreak.

Chrissie and Rodney

Key quote

'They were relieved they wouldn't have to face, more starkly than ever, the notion which fascinated and nagged and scared them: this notion of theirs that there were all kinds of possibilities open to us Hailsham students that weren't open to them.' (p.163)

Chrissie and Rodney are looked up to at the Cottages and Ruth is desperate to be accepted by them. They're friendly and helpful to new arrivals but also preoccupied with Hailsham and all its privileges. Kathy is wary of their motives and jealousy, illustrating how privilege creates social discord. Kathy mentions that Rodney talks a lot about 'reincarnation'(p.139), which mirrors the veteran couple's obsession with deferrals, suggesting a desperate desire for a better life.

THEMES, IDEAS & VALUES

Science, progress and ethics

Key quote

> 'After the war, in the early fifties, when the great breakthroughs in science followed one after the other so rapidly, there wasn't time to take stock, to ask the sensible questions.' (Miss Emily, p.257)

The novel presents a speculative version of England in which advancements in biomedicine have made human cloning possible and society harvests the clones' organs to cure diseases. Specifics of the science and structures underpinning the program are largely omitted from the novel and function as an abstract background to the plot. At first, readers only know that Kathy is a 'carer' for 'donors' (p.3), and while it's clear early on that life for Hailsham students is strange and sheltered, the reality that they are enslaved clones is only very slowly revealed. This positions readers to accept Kathy's humanity before fully comprehending she is a clone, encouraging them to have a critical response to the novel's society.

All levels of society are implicated in the clones' exploitation, from the scientists to the government who runs the system and the public who benefit. There's a brief mention of politicians and corporations who supported Miss Emily's philanthropic movement only to later allow crueller practices to resume when they retracted their support. The only people who appear to hold any concern for the clones' wellbeing are Miss Emily's 'small but very vocal movement' (p.256), but their claims of altruism are undermined by their repulsion. The secrecy and illegality revealed in the Morningdale scandal suggests society has constructed certain ethical beliefs, but the legitimacy of this is called into question by the choice to push the clones back into the 'shadows' rather than discontinuing the donor program (p.258).

The novel poses questions about how we measure benefits against detriments, warning us against being so spellbound by exciting new possibilities that we neglect to consider the ramifications of our actions. Miss Emily's comment that there's 'no way to reverse the process' reminds us that progress is largely irreversible (p.257). While the novel deals with cloning and organ harvesting, these concerns can be applied to science and progress more broadly. Breakthroughs in artificial intelligence, robotics and medicine are rapidly progressing and it's virtually impossible to predict what discoveries the future may hold. Innovations offer immense potential benefits to individuals and societies but may also produce a myriad of problems, such as wiping out some industries, depleting natural resources and causing ecological damage. The possibility of modifying human genetics also poses questions about citizenship and civil rights which challenge the relevance and efficacy of many long-held social systems and beliefs.

It's important to note that the clones are constructed as sympathetic, innocent and human victims, which undermines the notion that progress in science and technology is in itself a bad thing. The fault of this society is not necessarily that it made the clones, but *how* and *why* it made them, and why the public continues to support the practice after fear and regret have set in. Questions about moral responsibility aren't merely future-focused, either. Setting the story in an alternative recent history – rather than a parallel universe, fantastical past or speculative future – invites us to see the story world as an extension of our own. The beliefs, attitudes and values of the fictional society are the same ones that dominate our present. Ordinary citizens reap the benefits of the donor program while turning a blind eye to the atrocities it is responsible for, holding a mirror to the devasting impacts of our own apathy, denial and indifference. This correlates with issues related to science and consumerism, such as climate change, electronic waste, animal testing, sweatshops and child labour. Parallels can also be drawn to apathy about racism, sexism, homophobia, transphobia, poverty, refugees, war, political suppression and genocide.

Humans, humanity and dehumanisation

Key quote

'We took away your art because we thought it would reveal your souls. Or to put it more finely, we did to *prove you had souls at all.*' (Miss Emily, p.255)

Clones are described as 'copied' from 'normal' people (p.137), implying they're abnormal and not real humans. Given the clones eat, sleep, grow, think, feel, look and sound like 'normal' humans, we can infer that society classifies *human* by mode of conception and DNA. We have no reason to think the world of the novel is any different to ours, with the exception of human cloning. Therefore, we can assume IVF and twins exist, and there's no evidence in the novel that they are treated any differently. This undermines the logic of disregarding the clones' humanity, suggesting the entire belief system is fallacious.

Clinging to false beliefs allows society to rationalise and justify the donor program. If clones are aberrations, then they should be repelled. Because they're manufactured in a lab, they are merely synthetic biological products to be used and disposed of. If clones are not real, then neither is their pain and suffering. Underpinning this perspective are several widely held beliefs: *natural* is the ideal and *artificial* its moral opposite; humans are entitled to dominate and exploit non-human things; the ends justify the means. In examining what it really means to be human, the novel addresses each of these assumptions, undermining their logic and calling into question every real-world attitude, action and practice built upon them.

In opposition to society's views, Kathy and her friends are characterised with traits and experiences readers can relate to as authentically human. Aside from being infertile, the clones are anatomically and biologically human. Despite being genetic copies, each character has a unique personality. The narrative arc follows the trajectory of the human life cycle with Kathy and her friends moving through childhood to late adolescence to adulthood. They live and die, forge deep bonds, develop sexual urges, learn, grow, dream and grieve losses. Even Kathy's time as a carer is indicative of many ordinary people's experiences of adult life as the burdens of careers, responsibilities and social structures result in loneliness and monotony.

The melancholic tone of the narrative depends on readers sympathising with the clones. The tragedy of lives cut short, lost love and unfulfilled dreams appeals to common human desires. Despite their sombre lives, the clones embody qualities typically perceived as the best of human nature. Kathy is altruistic, self-aware and empathetic. Tommy is humble, kind and loyal. Ruth demonstrates growth and redemption. In contrast the 'normal' humans represent the worst of humanity: greed, selfishness, hubris, cruelty, corruption. Their beliefs and attitudes are shown to be hypocritical and illogical. The debate about clones' souls indicates some doubt about their own convictions and they willingly transplant cloned organs into their own bodies despite being repulsed by cloned people. Juxtaposing the attitudes and actions of clones and non-clones implies that the quality of being human is more than a body's genome or how a life is conceived. Instead, it is consciousness and sentience, the capacity for empathy, self-awareness and insight.

Identity and belonging

Key quote

> 'Nevertheless, we all of us, to varying degrees, believed that when you saw the person you were copied from, you'd get *some* insight into who you were deep down, and maybe too, you'd see something of what your life held in store.' (pp.137–8)

Ideas about identity and belonging emphasise the clones' humanness and make the differences between clones and non-clones seem arbitrary. Ishiguro structures the narrative as a journey from childhood to adulthood and has embedded nuances of biological development and identity formation into the characters' behaviours, perspectives and dialogue. Like all children, Hailsham students develop the foundation of their identity from the circumstances of their daily lives. Their self-perception hangs on being a collective unit of 'students' who belong to 'Hailsham' (p.43). They believe they're privileged because they are told as much and their physical surroundings support the notion. Nevertheless, much of what they learn is contradictory: they are 'special' (p.43) but also 'different' from other people (p.36); guardians and other staff 'joke and laugh' with them and call them 'sweetheart' (p.36) but the students are also geographically isolated, surrounded by fences and unwelcome in society. Because children are trusting and think literally, they're unable to reconcile these contradictions and consequently absorb the paradoxes into their identity, so that being both privileged and subordinate become the core tenets of their identity.

As they grow up, Kathy and her friends go through a typical human adolescence. Despite being infertile, they go through puberty and develop sexual urges. They become more inquisitive as the desire for independence kicks in and they become increasingly self-conscious as the need for peer approval overrides the desire to please adults. Moving to the Cottages correlates with leaving school and moving out of home as typical young adult milestones. Kathy misses the guardians and Ruth works hard to prove her maturity, suggesting fairly normal experiences of being separated from caregivers. Many common rites of passage are represented, including making new friends, having sex, road trips, crushes and heartbreak. Many of these experiences unsettle characters' identities and intensify feelings of connection and isolation. This transition into adulthood parallels the experiences of many in modern society. Friends drift away as they move on to training and careers, and identities become tied to a person's professional status and how fulfilled and successful they feel.

The parallels between the coming-of-age plot and common human life stages invites comparison between the characters and real-life humans. On one hand, similarities emphasise the clones' humanity while conveying that the need to belong and understand oneself are central to the human experience. On the other, differences emphasise what's missing from the clones' lives: family, loving parental figures, opportunities to develop unique talents and interests, career choices, further education, having their own home, financial independence, getting married, having their own families. Kathy doesn't express any direct thoughts or feelings about what's lacking from her life and there are several ways this could be interpreted. One could argue that depriving someone of essential human needs is cruel and Kathy's silence on the matter indicates ignorance, denial or brainwashing. Alternatively, it could be argued that Kathy's ability to overcome this deprivation is testament to human resilience and adaptability.

The depiction of recognised identity-formation processes also taps into the nature versus nurture debate – that is, whether who we are is determined by genes or environment. Despite being shut off from human society in an artificial environment, the clones still seek self-understanding and connection, implying these needs are hardwired into human DNA. Also, Kathy's attempts to make sense of her relationships endorse the view that humans are biologically social animals. On the other hand, the bildungsroman structure implies that Kathy's adult perceptions and values are a result of her childhood, which supports the belief that identity and personality are also influenced by environmental factors. Hailsham manipulates students' worldview to ensure the role of organ donor is absorbed into their identities. None of the characters questions their obligation to follow the path set for them, reinforcing the view that social factors have powerful impacts on identity.

Despite students accepting their prescribed identities, many struggle with poor self-image which manifests through insecurity, low self-esteem and vivid fantasies. Curiosity about 'possibles' is a clear example (p.136). While attitudes vary from obsessive to dismissive, the persistence of the theory suggests that having no family or knowledge of their model affects their sense of self and belonging. For many, finding their 'possible' would connect them to history and the world, as proof they are part of something bigger and not simply disposable anomalies. Seeking possibles could be expressing a need to know that, if their circumstances were different, they would have had the capacity to lead meaningful lives. Similar desires underpin talk about 'dream futures' (p.140) and deferrals (pp.150–2), suggesting that understanding one's potential is essential to understanding oneself.

These fantasies also imply an inner struggle to understand oneself as a separate and distinct being, which is made particularly difficult for students who have been taught to see themselves as belonging to a collective group with a shared purpose. Being 'special' at Hailsham relates only to donating organs and not to students' individual traits (p.43). Opportunities to develop talents are limited to sports and producing art for the Gallery and Exchanges; this conditions students to value health and altruism, supporting their prescribed identities as non-autonomous providers of body parts. Tommy's struggle with art exposes the cruelty of suppressing children and enforcing rigid expectations; however, the novel also disrupts the dominant notion that individuality and absolute freedom are essential to fulfilling lives and stable identities. Ruth and Tommy both face death with a peaceful dignity that reminds us that every life contains limitations and unfulfilled dreams. Kathy makes the most of the hand life dealt her, choosing to be grateful for her relationships rather than wallowing in all that she could not be. The novel paints excessive social control in a chilling light but, at the same time, the ability of some characters to find fulfilment and the sympathetic portrayal of their kindness and humility are elements that undermine simplistic debates about individualistic versus collective goals.

Key point

In the end, life for donors and carers is lonely, exhausting and traumatising. Childhood friends fade away and die. Even Kathy's romance with Tommy is short-lived and they both must face death alone. This conflicts with Hailsham students being raised with a strong sense of belonging and loyalty to other clones, which implies the need to belong was used against the students, to make them obedient and agreeable, rather than to truly fulfil their need for love and connection. This relates to the title, evoking a plea and demand that encapsulates the human need to belong.

Death, mortality and survival

Key quote

> 'I keep thinking about this river somewhere, with the water moving really fast. And these two people in the water, trying to hold onto each other, holding on as hard as they can, but in the end it's just too much. The current's too strong. They've got to let go, drift apart. That's how I think it is with us. It's a shame, Kath, because we've loved each other all our lives. But in the end, we can't stay together forever.' (Tommy, p.277)

Facing death and the impermanence of life is a central theme of the novel. The clones' forced participation in organ harvesting essentially issues them a death sentence before they are born. Society appears to justify clones' murders on the premise that it gave clones life and these lives are not natural occurrences. In contradiction of this view, the characters grapple with their mortality in ways that validate the authenticity, dignity and value of their lives.

The novel suggests that beliefs about mortality influence how people both live their lives and approach their deaths. For every human, death is an inevitable reality. Self-preservation instincts combined with anxieties about mortality are often managed through beliefs about transcendence. Many cultures and religions have immortality or afterlife myths, which can subdue death's grim finality and provide comfort by promising there's something more or better on the other side. Many people also seek out symbolic immortality in the hope of living on through memory. Common strategies include devoting one's life to a cause or career that leaves a lasting impact, creating art or literature that survives after one's death, or having children to continue one's heritage. Other than a brief mention of Rodney's interest in reincarnation, the clones don't discuss what happens after death. However, Ishiguro's choice to structure the novel in an autobiographical form endows Kathy's character with a desire to immortalise proof of her existence and preserve her loved ones' memories. Likewise, her dedication to her patients as a carer could be viewed as an attempt to leave her mark on the world by making a difference in other people's lives.

Kathy's attitude to death is much the same as her attitude to life. She accepts what's out of her control, keeps her emotions contained and shows compassion for others' suffering. Underpinning these attitudes are the values of altruism, servitude, loyalty and self-sacrifice. Through Kathy's sympathetic characterisation these values are conveyed as admirable and desirable. However, there's a paradox at work here, given these are the same values promoted at Hailsham to control and indoctrinate students. In one sense, it appears Kathy has co-opted Hailsham's belief system into something more virtuous. Then again, she never questions what she has been taught about her existence.

Kathy grows up with certain beliefs about the world, which are mostly based on faith rather than fact. Aspects of Hailsham's culture and ideology emphasise the relationship between faith and belief, drawing attention to how this can be exploited. Through students' confinement and the worldview they're taught, the world outside is imbued with a mythical otherworldliness – a 'fantasy land' (p.66) – and the lives of non-cloned humans are perceived as being the stuff of dreams, as evidenced by the 'dream futures' (p.140). Ironically, those being saved do not view the clones as heroic or remarkable, which indicates that the beliefs instilled in the clones are merely a tool of manipulation.

Given the centrality of death and mortality to the novel's plot and many themes, the way characters talk and think about death is significant. Clones only refer to dying as 'completing' and the word *death* is omitted from the novel entirely. In contrast to regular people, clones' untimely deaths are unambiguous certainties, inflicted on them by others with premediated intent, and intrinsically tied to how they understand their existence. While it seems they willingly submit to suffering and death, the characters still exhibit human fears and anxieties. The deferrals theory reflects a human desire to hold off death, Ruth seeks absolution from Kathy and Tommy so she can die in peace and Tommy breaks up with Kathy to ease her suffering and preserve his dignity.

Freedom and power

Key quote

'Tommy thought it possible the guardians had, throughout all our years at Hailsham, timed very carefully and deliberately everything they told us, so that we were always just too young to understand properly the latest piece of information. But of course we'd take it in at some level, so that before long all this stuff was there in our heads without us ever having examined it properly.' (p.81)

In the story world clones have no rights, freedom or agency. They don't even have autonomy over their own bodies – they are literally someone else's legal and material property. One of the most chilling aspects of this is the characters' passive acceptance of these circumstances. We see no evidence of characters questioning their fate or attempting to escape. As a carer, Kathy drives around the country unsupervised, no physical boundaries preventing her from taking off and starting her own life. The fact that she never considers this demonstrates how social exclusion and ideology can create invisible chains that become deeply entrenched in the psyches of oppressed people.

Narrating the story through Kathy's point of view emphasises how mechanisms of oppression have become normalised in her mind. As readers slowly piece things together and see things Kathy cannot, it becomes clear that everything about Hailsham is a *sham* and the very nature of this upbringing is central to the students' indoctrination. While Miss Emily may claim the philanthropic schools were intended to shield students from the 'horrors' inflicted on other clones and provide a 'cultured' education in 'wonderful surroundings' (pp.255–6), in practice every aspect of these institutions is an insidious control tactic which supports the goals and structures of the donor program. Students might not understand what Miss Lucy means when she obscurely mentions it's a good thing 'fences at Hailsham aren't electrified' because 'you get terrible accidents sometimes' (p.77), but this suggests that the clones growing up in 'deplorable conditions' elsewhere in the country (p.255) do try to escape and suffer greatly for it. The illusion of privilege and freedom at Hailsham is a form of psychological confinement, which is perhaps even more sinister than physical restraints. Two important ideas are raised here: firstly, if people can be convinced that something terrible is good for them, they do not need to be forced to participate; secondly, if humanitarian programs merely try to make atrocities more tolerable rather than fighting the root cause of injustice, they become complicit in perpetuating the forces of disempowerment.

The culture of Hailsham exploits children's naivety to create a false reality that becomes virtually impossible to question as they grow up. Everything seems nice on the surface but all lessons, routines and customs enforce a doctrine of subservience through common propaganda techniques. Half-truths, intentional vagueness and lies are used to teach students about the world and the donor program, slowly drip-feeding information to encourage gradual acceptance of an unacceptable idea. The brutality of forced organ harvesting is obscured through positive connotations of the euphemisms 'donation', 'carer' and 'completing', which are also virtue words reinforcing desired values and which are repeated ad nauseam so they appear to be an undeniable truth. Students are repeatedly told they are 'special' (p.43) which is a form of doublespeak, a euphemism that deliberately obscures or reverses meaning, portraying organ donation as a great honour, and minimising fear and doubt. Promoting sameness and students as a collective unit instils intense loyalty and groupthinking. The focus on health, through regular medical check-ups, playing sport and anti-smoking messages, appears to be in students' best interest but is in fact teaching them that their bodies do not belong to them and is a form of behaviour modification.

The possibility of rebellion or escape is prevented through censorship, surveillance and coercion. Segregating students from the outside world, redacting books and restricting the curriculum avoids exposure to ideas which might undermine the school's doctrines. This is reinforced by a culture of silence and secrecy that discourages open discussion of taboo topics. The buildings and grounds limit opportunities for private conversations and create a sense among students that they are always being watched. Coercion doesn't occur through typical methods of violence or the threat of banishment. Instead, fear of the woods and the outside world prevents students wanting to leave, while the fear of peer exclusion promotes self-regulation. If doubts or questions arise, life is comfortable, safe and peaceful enough that students are unlikely to suspect anything sinister. Even as an adult, when Tommy suggests they had been taught about donations in a calculated way, Kathy doubts the guardians could have been 'that crafty' (p.81).

The culture around 'creating' (p.16) is one of the most powerful indoctrination strategies used. Pushing students to develop and value the same talent discourages individuality and the desire for autonomy. The goal of creating is not individual artistic expression but producing work for Exchanges and Madame's Gallery, in order to predispose students to giving and donating. The perpetual cycle of creating and giving ties students' self-worth to producing things that are desired by others. Depending on each other to obtain treasures for their 'collections' (p.38) fosters obligation and mutual reliance, perhaps in preparation for becoming carers. Guardians decide arbitrarily how many tokens each piece is worth, normalising students' lack of agency and reinforcing the guardians' (and the state's) absolute power. Students' best work isn't available to their peers and is given to Madame, reinforcing clones' inferiority to non-clones and acclimatising students to giving away their most precious things without expecting anything in return.

The relationship between power and knowledge is evident in Hailsham students' beliefs about themselves and the world. As effective as Hailsham's system of indoctrination is, we see many examples of students wanting to know more. Questions, speculation and attempting to fill gaps in knowledge on topics such as sex, possibles, the Gallery and deferrals imply that the capacity for independent thought has not been completely eliminated. However, ignorance and censorship prevent students finding truthful or satisfying answers, often leading to fanciful theories and rumours that reinforce their ignorance. Without access to alternative ideas and information, students have little choice but to accept the ideology of Hailsham as reality and internalise their oppression. They believe they are inferior to other humans and have no place in the human world so that, even after they leave Hailsham, they never form relationships with non-clones and continue to live on the edges of society.

Despite the prevalence of passivity and conformity, students are not wholly content slaves. Characters deal with and respond to their disempowerment in various ways that suggest underlying insecurities and dissatisfaction. Fantasising about 'dream futures' (p.140) provides some students with a form of escapism, while talk of deferrals offers hope that they can experience at least a few more years of ordinary life. Ruth's manipulative behaviour allows her to feel in control, while Kathy achieves this by actively preserving her memories, reclaiming some power by placing significance on the one thing 'no one can take away' (p.281). While the clones accept their fate, they do so in different ways. Some endure caring and donating with a crushing hopelessness, while others become stoically resolved. Kathy takes pride in her job as carer, finding small pleasures where she can. Accepting what she can and cannot control alleviates feelings of powerlessness, allowing her to find value and meaning in her life.

Key point

The fictional society is represented as corrupt through its conflicting values. Compassion and the dignity of life underlie the desire to cure diseases; however, society places more value on human supremacy, progress, control and personal gain, which is used to justify oppressing, enslaving and killing clones. The clones are taught to value altruism and humility, despite these values not being upheld by the government, institutions or the general public. This conveys how ideology can be manipulated as a tool of control. The novel promotes equality, diversity, friendship, human connection and the dignity of all life, while questioning the values that underpin egotism, apathy about injustice and others' suffering, prejudice and hierarchical social structures.

DIFFERENT INTERPRETATIONS

Different interpretations arise from different responses to a text. Over time, a text will evoke a wide range of responses from its readers, who may come from various social or cultural groups and live in very different places and historical periods. Responses by critics and reviewers can be published in newspapers, journals and books, both online and in print. They can also be expressed in discussions among readers in the media, classrooms, book groups and so on.

While there is no single correct reading or interpretation of a text, it is important to understand that an interpretation is more than a personal opinion – it is the justification of a point of view on the text. To present an interpretation of a text based on your point of view, you must use a logical argument and support it with relevant evidence from the text.

The critics' viewpoints

Ishiguro has said *Never Let Me Go* was intended as a story of friendship between young people coming to the realisation that time is short. Cloning and organ harvesting were incorporated late in the writing process as a device for compressing time and foregrounding characters' mortality (Adams 2005, Film Independent 2010, Ishiguro 2005b). Many reviewers and critics have read the novel along these lines, such as *The Telegraph*'s Theo Tait who describes it as 'parable about mortality' (Tait 2005), and critic M John Harrison who interprets the cloning debate as a 'sleight of hand', arguing the novel is about how and why humans survive in the most harrowing circumstances (Harrison 2005). *The Independent*'s Andrew Barrow interprets the science fiction elements as a device for throwing 'light on ordinary human life'. In contrast to Harrison, Barrow reads Kathy's story as allegorising how we're all 'copycats and mimics who acquire our mannerisms from the TV and cinema screens, even advertisements, as much as from our elders and betters' and that to some extent all our lives are set out for us (Barrow 2005).

Many readers and reviewers have questioned why the clones never try to break free. Ishiguro has responded by saying he never set out to write a dystopian story of escape; he was interested in why people don't always run away from hardship and the fact no one can escape their mortality (Film Independent 2010, Ishiguro 2005b, Wroe 2005). While dystopian themes might not have been Ishiguro's primary concern, the inclusion of dystopian elements (see 'Genre, Structure & Language') means many have interpreted the novel in relation to how it performs in this tradition.

Scholar John Mullen describes the novel as working 'at a tangent' to dystopian fiction due to Ishiguro's evasions of generic expectations by setting the narrative in a realistic past, the subtlety of the science fiction elements and a protagonist who doesn't rebel (Mullen 2010, p.105). Mullen argues Kathy's fatalistic 'avoidance of protest' prompts readers familiar with the genre to 'associate individuality with resistance' (Mullen 2010, p.106). He describes the Hailsham students' upbringings as placing such stringent limitations on individuality that they cannot imagine any life or identity other than the one prescribed to them. Consequently, they cannot see their own enslavement or any need for resistance.

Similarly, literary theorist Kalina Maleska identifies characters' conflict with a hierarchical class system that suppresses their individuality as a hallmark feature of dystopian fiction. However, she argues the novel subverts the dystopian tradition of warning against technological advancements which might suppress freedom and enable dictatorships. She claims that 'rather than cautioning about technological development, [the novel] actually cautions about fear of technological development'. She interprets the clones as 'victims of the human technophobic views' (Maleska 2019, p.134) who are isolated, not because they are dangerous, but because of society's irrational fears. Maleska interprets Madame and Miss Emily as clinging to the past, believing progress has made the world cruel and harsh and failing to see that the cruelty is a result of their own actions.

In a review in *The American Journal of Bioethics*, Daniel Vorhaus describes the novel as a love story that illuminates the 'absurdity and irrationality' of 'the fear of the unknown' (Vorhaus 2007, p.100). As a lawyer specialising in bioethics, Vorhaus advocates prohibiting human reproductive cloning in the current climate but believes safe and ethical human cloning is plausible in the future. This position informs his interpretation of Kathy and the students as inverting common stereotypes of clones as terrifying 'boogeymen' (Vorhaus 2007, p.99). More broadly, he interprets the novel as a warning against fear and closed-mindedness so that we can be accepting and humane when the first human clone is inevitably born.

Other scholars have read the novel as a bildungsroman, focusing on ideas about agency and identity. Ji Eun Lee describes the role of individual development in the traditional Western bildungsroman as being 'grounded in a sense of agency, that is, the ability to direct one's own action and decision' and promoting goals of self-formation and maturity in order 'to find a harmonious conjunction' with one's social system (Lee 2019, pp.270–1). Lee interprets Kathy's narration as subverting this tradition by conveying how following the path set by society results in an 'emptying' of her 'self'. She interprets Kathy's narration as 'severed from her present consciousness' because we never know where she is while narrating and describes the style as 'a chronological report of past events and other characters' behaviors, neither reflecting deep understanding of a certain moment nor giving us any clue to her profound meditation on her past dreams, wishes and perspectives' (Lee 2019, p.283).

Titus Levy reads the novel as a 'dissensual bildungsroman', a contemporary subgenre that 'narrates the individual's assimilation into the social order, while simultaneously protesting the oppressive social conditions that the state forces on its subjects'. Levy interprets the use of an autobiographical form as making Kathy's narration a 'courageous act of protest by giving a marginalized minority a form of humanistic expression' which gives voice to her trauma and exposes how atrocities are normalised and hidden in everyday life. Levy describes society's apathy as a 'denial of moral responsibility' similar to how many people turn a blind eye to 'mass suffering that occurs in distant, unfamiliar regions of the world' even though they have 'more than a passing connection to the exploitative processes that subject others to pain and degradation' (Levy 2011, p.14).

Mimi Wong raises similar ideas in her analysis of the novel as a 'racial metaphor', offering an alternative reading informed by her personal context as a person of colour. She acknowledges the omission of concrete physical characteristics means many readers would assume characters are white, just as the 2010 film adaptation did; however, she argues it's possible to read the characters as non-white because they are subjected to a system of marginalisation and assimilation that 'reframes the history of imperialism as a conflict between those considered human and those who are not' (Wong 2018). Wong cites Kathy's experiences of objectification by Madame as familiar to people of colour and points out that contemporary practices of organ trafficking, commercial surrogacy, forced labour, prostitution and indentured servitude predominantly exploit non-white people and countries.

Scholar Matava Vichiensing also interprets the novel as an examination of 'othering' practices that marginalise people by relegating them to an inferior out-group. In contrast to Wong's analysis, Vichiensing considers how the novel reflects experiences of groups who are excluded based on 'gender, sex, race, social class, or religion' (Vichiensing 2017, p.127). Vichiensing identifies three key mechanisms of othering being at work in the novel. Firstly, clones are 'indoctrinated' at Hailsham; secondly they are 'objectified' through dehumanising perceptions of their bodies as objects; and, thirdly, the illusion of privilege at Hailsham promotes 'assimilation' by conditioning them to adopt the values, beliefs and behaviours of the dominant group despite being excluded from it (Vichiensing 2017, p.127).

Two interpretations

Interpretation 1: *Never Let Me Go* positions readers to condemn human indifference to cruelty and injustice.

Never Let Me Go represents real-world attitudes to cruelty and injustice. Narrating the story through the first-person voice of a clone encourages readers to feel empathy for victims of injustice; while featuring non-clone characters only in minor roles, with little insight into their perspectives, encourages us to respond critically to those who ignore or benefit from the mistreatment and oppression of others.

Set in an alternate reality, in the style of a coming-of-age narrative, Kathy's account of her relatively carefree schooldays has a strong focus on friendships and schoolyard dynamics. Her anecdotes invite us to relate to her young life and the ups and downs of growing up. The first-person narrative style and level of detail in Kathy's expression of her curiosity, hopes and fears reinforce this sense of relatability. Readers are positioned to empathise with the clones so, with the revelation of their fate as organ donors, we are horrified by the cruelty of a system that mercilessly exploits a group of people whose thoughts and emotions are not so different from our own.

In contrast, the ordinary (non-clone) public is almost entirely omitted from the novel; most of the readers' insight into the dominant society's perceptions of clones comes from Miss Emily's dialogue in Chapter Twenty-two. Ironically, this is the group to which readers belong. By positioning us to identify with the clones and keeping the non-clones at a distance, Ishiguro encourages us to view the non-clones' attitudes and, in turn, our own attitudes, with a critical eye. Although the reasoning for organ harvesting is explained and portrayed as understandable as Miss Emily describes the 'overwhelming concern … that their own children, their spouses, their parents, their friends, did not die from cancer' (p.258), the novel's narration from the clones' perspective heavily emphasises the darker consequences arising from this. The system relies on broader society tolerating and refusing to challenge it; non-clones make excuses for the deep injustice done to the clones, in order to continue to reap the benefits.

When confronted with the injustice of the situation, the non-clones' reaction suggests cognitive dissonance: common human values such as kindness and equality conflict with organ harvesting and society's cruelty to the clones. Even though people try to ease this conflict by rationalising their behaviour, they still feel guilty, so they refuse to see the clones as equal human beings, and send them 'back in the shadows' (p.259) to ease their own discomfort. Miss Emily's behaviour in Chapter Twenty-two demonstrates this: she is preoccupied with her bedside cabinet while she is dashing Tommy and Kathy's dreams of a deferral, and tells them that their lives 'must now run the course that's been set' (p.261). Despite her alleged sympathy, she does not give them much regard and her distracted refusal to help her former students to avoid an early death is, from a readers' perspective, a reprehensible moral failure.

The irony of the guardians' benevolence while supporting the exploitation of the clones is similarly unsettling. Many treat the clones with the affection that teachers show their students, but despite being aware of their charges' tragic fate, they do not help the clones escape their future. Even Miss Lucy, despite her clear anger and discomfort, never does anything to change the system or free the students. Her attempt to explain organ harvesting to them only leaves them 'puzzled' (p.80) and does nothing to change their fate, suggesting perhaps her own powerlessness against a system that has almost universal support.

Ishiguro ends Kathy's narrative with a moment that emphasises her humanity, as she thinks of her childhood and mourns Tommy, at a point not long before she will become a donor herself. Readers' awareness of Kathy's destiny prompts us to imagine the story continuing and to picture her painful and dehumanising death. Thus, we are left with the image of a world that will continue to create, mutilate and kill people for selfish ends, positioning us to reflect on the brutal consequences of ordinary people's apathy and indifference, and the denial and tolerance of injustice.

Interpretation 2: *Never Let Me Go* demonstrates how social systems can prevent individuals from living up to their potential.

Never Let Me Go illustrates how society can inhibit and restrict people's lives. Using the clones as representative of the ordinary person confined by social and legal structures, the novel exemplifies how social norms can prevent individuals from reaching their potential.

The clone characters in the novel are symbolic representations of humanity. Kathy's coming-of-age arc and intimate narrative voice, detailing her deepest desires and vulnerabilities (e.g. her frank discussion of her fears surrounding sexuality), as well as her struggles with love and loss, evoke the universal experience of growing up and the life experiences that everyone must face. Similarly, the wider society depicted in the novel, despite its futuristic and dystopian elements, reflects the real world. Closely resembling English society in the 1990s, the settings of *Never Let Me Go* are familiar: Kathy refers to real geographic locations (e.g. Norfolk and Kingsfield), as well as British cultural icons such as Sherlock Holmes. Aside from these overt ties to reality, settings such as Hailsham and the recovery centres resemble the real-world institutions of boarding schools and hospices, encouraging us to view this world as a reflection of our own.

Ishiguro uses the major difference between *Never Let Me Go*'s society and our own world – the use of human cloning for the purpose of organ harvesting – to highlight the mechanisms that social systems can use to control citizens, restricting their freedom and opportunities. The brainwashing at Hailsham, in which children are drip-fed information about their terrible future – 'told and not told' (p.79) – should appear shocking. However, described through Kathy's young eyes along with the other strange secrets and mysteries of childhood, the information is relayed in a somewhat matter-of-fact manner, as if it is normal. When Miss Lucy attempts to explain to the students their future as organ donors, they are more surprised at her 'outburst' than her actual words (p.80) – which are horrifying to readers, who haven't been indoctrinated in the ways of this society's dystopian medical system.

This continues throughout the novel, with frequent evidence of social norms that should be disconcerting but are treated as a matter of course. For example, a donor about to make a fourth donation is 'treated with special respect' (p.273), and the clones' thoughts of surviving the fate society has allotted them are acknowledged only as dreams. All these norms act insidiously to maintain the status quo, supporting the system of raising clones for organ harvesting, and allowing it to remain unchallenged. Through this one element of overt horror in an otherwise serene and comfortable world of relatable characters and realistic settings, readers are encouraged to consider the social norms – those taught in our schools, relayed among peers or embedded in institutions and cultures – that invisibly shape our own behaviours and beliefs.

The non-clones' attitudes towards the clones are similarly jarring, and reflect discriminatory attitudes in our own society, demonstrating the dehumanising and harmful impacts of prejudice. Miss Emily's unexpected admission to feeling 'revulsion' when looking at her young charges (p.264), Madame recoiling from the students as though they were 'spiders' (p.35) and Ruth's outburst saying that they were modelled from 'trash' (p.164) are all momentous and upsetting incidents, stark reminders of the clones' inferiority. Here, parallels can be seen with real life: aspects of identity such as ethnicity, class, culture, sexuality and gender affect access to education, cultural capital and social mobility. The clones growing up with dreams that will never be fulfilled mirrors the lack of opportunities for underprivileged groups in our own society, which limits people's choices and ability to fulfill their potential.

The horror and realism of the dystopian world of *Never Let Me Go* shines a light on how socially constructed perceptions of reality can limit independent thought and maintain a status quo, no matter how oppressive. As we see the characters' perspectives, behaviours and fates being shaped by their society, and not by their own decisions and aspirations, readers are invited to consider how we ourselves have been conditioned to accept and value the rules, beliefs and systems of our own society, and the ways in which we so often unthinkingly adhere to social conventions that limit our freedom and the freedom of others.

QUESTIONS & ANSWERS

This section focuses on your own analytical writing on the text, and gives you strategies for producing high-quality responses in your coursework and exam essays.

Essay writing – an overview

An essay on a literary work is a formal and serious piece of writing that presents your point of view on the text, usually in response to a given topic. Your 'point of view' in an essay is your interpretation of the meaning of the text's language, structure, characters, situations and events, supported by detailed analysis of textual evidence.

Analyse – don't summarise

In your essays it is important to avoid simply summarising what happens in a text.

- A **summary** is a description or paraphrase (retelling in different words) of the characters and events. For example: 'Macbeth has a horrifying vision of a dagger dripping with blood before he goes to murder King Duncan.'
- An **analysis** is an explanation of the real meaning or significance that lies 'beneath' the text's words (and images, for a film). For example: 'Macbeth's vision of a bloody dagger shows how deeply uneasy he is about the violent act he is contemplating, and conveys his sense that supernatural forces are impelling him to act.'

A limited amount of summary is sometimes necessary to let your reader know which part of the text you wish to discuss. However, always keep this to a minimum and follow it immediately with your analysis of what this part of the text is really telling us.

Plan your essay

Carefully plan your essay so that you have a clear idea of what you are going to say. The plan ensures that your ideas flow logically, that your argument remains consistent and that you stay on the topic. An essay plan should be a list of **brief dot points** covering no more than half a page.

- Include your central argument or main contention – a concise statement of your overall response to the topic.
- Write three or four dot points for each paragraph, indicating the main idea and evidence/examples from the text. Note that in your essay you will need to *expand* on these points and *analyse* the evidence.

Structure your essay

An essay is a complete, self-contained piece of writing. It has a clear beginning (the introduction), middle (several body paragraphs) and end (the last paragraph or conclusion). It must also have a central argument that runs throughout, linking each paragraph to form a coherent whole. See examples of introductions and conclusions in the 'Analysing a sample topic' and 'Sample answer' sections.

The introduction establishes your overall response to the topic. It includes your main contention and outlines the main evidence you will refer to in the course of the essay. Write your introduction *after* you have done a plan and *before* you write the rest of the essay.

The body paragraphs argue your case – they present evidence from the text and explain how this evidence supports your argument. Each body paragraph needs:

- a strong **topic sentence** (usually the first sentence) that states the main point being made in the paragraph
- **evidence** from the text, including some brief quotations
- **analysis** of the textual evidence, with **explanation** of its significance and how it supports your argument
- **links back to the topic** in one or more statements, usually towards the end of the paragraph.

Connect the body paragraphs so that your discussion flows smoothly. Use some linking words and phrases such as 'similarly' and 'on the other hand', though don't start every paragraph like this. Another strategy is to use a significant word from the last sentence of one paragraph in the first sentence of the next.

Use key terms from the topic – or synonyms for them – throughout, so the relevance of your discussion to the topic is always clear.

The conclusion ties everything together and finishes the essay. It includes strong statements that emphasise your central argument and provide a clear response to the topic.

Avoid simply restating the points made earlier in the essay – this will end on a very flat note and imply that you have run out of ideas and vocabulary. The conclusion should be a logical extension of what you have written, not just a repetition or summary of it. Writing an effective conclusion can be a challenge. Try using these tips:

- Start by linking back to the final sentence of the second-last paragraph, rather than leaping to your main contention straight away – this helps your writing to flow.
- Use synonyms and expressions with equivalent meanings to vary your vocabulary. This allows you to reinforce your line of argument without being repetitive.
- When planning your essay, think of one or two broad statements or observations about the text's wider meaning. These should be related to the topic and your overall argument. Keep them for the conclusion, since they will give you something 'new' to say but still follow logically from your discussion. The introduction will be focused on the topic, but the conclusion can present a wider view of the text.

Essay topics

1. Explore how one character's experiences at Hailsham had a lasting impact on them.
2. How does Kathy's acceptance of her fate convey her perspective as a clone?
3. "… any place beyond Hailsham was like a fantasy land."
   Examine the role of fantasy in the novel.
4. How does the style of Kathy's narration convey ideas about memories?
5. '*Never Let Me Go* shines a light on the best and worst of humanity.'
   Discuss.
6. "Once I'm able to have a quieter life, in whichever centre they send me to, I'll have Hailsham with me, safely in my head, and that'll be something no one can take away."
   How does Kathy's attachment to Hailsham develop ideas about identity?
7. Kazuo Ishiguro has said he wanted 'to write a story in which every reader might find an echo of his or her own life'.
   Discuss how your interpretation of a theme is influenced by recognising an echo of your own life in the novel.
8. "Your life must now run the course that's been set for it."
   How does this quote exemplify Miss Emily's attitudes and beliefs?
9. Discuss how the novel challenged you to rethink a belief or assumption you previously held.
10. "What I really wanted, I suppose, was to get straight all the things that happened between me and Tommy and Ruth after we grew up and left Hailsham."
    Discuss how the relationship between Kathy, Tommy and Ruth shapes your interpretation of the novel.

Vocabulary for writing on *Never Let Me Go*

Agency: ability to act or exert power in one's life.

Alienation: feeling or being disconnected from society or a group.

Allegory: story that functions symbolically.

Altruism: acting selflessly for the benefit of others.

Assimilation: the process of marginalised groups adopting the behaviour and values of the dominant group.

Autonomy: freedom to determine one's own choices and actions.

Defamiliarization: literary device in which familiar things are made strange.

Dystopian fiction: branch of science fiction that depicts an imaginary world in which everything is bad, e.g. a corrupt and oppressive society (opposite of a utopia).

Hierarchy: organisational system that ranks people in terms of status or authority.

Human experience: common experiences of a human being (e.g. birth, growing up, loss, grief, love, aspiration, death).

Ideology: system of shared beliefs.

Objectification: dehumanising a person by treating them as an object.

Oppression: cruel or unjust treatment by an authority which limits rights and freedoms.

Other: a person or group excluded or alienated by social attitudes and norms.

Othering: the process of excluding or alienating people who don't belong to the dominant group.

Speculative fiction: fiction that uses non-realist elements and conjecture.

Analysing a sample topic

Explore how one character's experiences at Hailsham had a lasting impact on them.

This question requires you to discuss the characterisation of Kathy, Tommy or Ruth by examining how the representation of their childhood experiences contributes to their character arc. You should consider how the character changes and make clear links between examples from their childhood and later years to prove a connection.

In discussing childhood experiences you could consider the character's relationships, internal and external conflicts, childhood needs that were met and not met, and accomplishments and highlights, as well as any traumatic events they experienced, and things they learned about themselves and the world. The question explicitly refers to 'Hailsham', so it's important to consider how the setting and culture of Hailsham shapes the experiences. You might examine how confinement, indoctrination, norms and ideology influence both the childhood experience and the character's future outlook, choices and identity.

To discuss how experiences had a 'lasting impact' you need to address both the 'impact' (the effect or influence) and how it is 'lasting' (sustained or recurring for a long time). It's wise to choose childhood events you can prove had an impact at various stages of the character's life. To demonstrate insight, you should consider significant impacts rather than trivial ones, and be able to discuss the ramifications for the character in adulthood. Impacts could be positive or negative. Negative impacts might include limiting beliefs, damage to their psyche, warped views, unachieved potential, fears, feeling powerless or being traumatised. Positive impacts might include resilience, coping mechanisms, overcoming adversity or finding joy and fulfilment. Be mindful that some impacts are not exclusively positive or negative and it might be worth considering both benefits and detriments.

A well-developed response will also consider how the experiences and impacts relate to broader themes, issues and contexts. When analysing examples you should consider elements of character construction – remember, characters are not real people, they are fictional creations characterised directly and indirectly through techniques which include speech, actions, thoughts and relationships. Complex characters will embody contradictions and have nuanced personalities. Dynamic characters will undergo transformations of mindset, values, goals and circumstances. It may also be useful to consider how symbolism and motif emphasise elements of characterisation and themes.

Sample introduction

> Kazuo Ishiguro's *Never Let Me Go* is a tragedy of lost hopes and dreams following the lives of human clones bred for the purpose of having their organs harvested. Kathy, Tommy and Ruth grow up in an insular bubble inside Hailsham boarding school, oblivious to the full extent of their dehumanised existence. The cruelty of the school's deception is highlighted through Tommy's experiences with Hailsham's culture of art and creating. His lack of talent initially alienates him from his peers but he overcomes this when disillusioned guardian Miss Lucy challenges Hailsham's doctrines by telling him it is okay to be different. Nonetheless, he leaves Hailsham with the unshakeable belief that students' art has a profound importance to the world outside. This evolves into fanciful theories and years of cultivating false hope, only to eventually learn that everything he believed about himself and his life was built on a ruthless lie.

Body paragraphs

Paragraph 1: The culture of Hailsham and mythical prestige of Madame's Gallery establishes a collective belief that students' art has some mysterious importance.

- Miss Emily and guardians promote an illusion of prestige: 'We were all very special, being Hailsham students' (p.43).
- Creating is central to everyday life and Tommy's ostracism reinforces artistic aptitude as defining one's worth: 'How much you were liked and respected, had to do with how good you were at "creating"' (p.16).
- Work taken by Madame implies a link between being 'special' and their art: 'most distinguished honour' (Miss Emily, p.39).
- The pomp and secrecy surrounding Madame's visits enhances prestigious and mythical qualities: 'lead-up to her arrival began weeks before'; 'The billiards room would get closed during this period' (p.33).

Paragraph 2: Tommy's talks with Miss Lucy reinforce the Gallery myth and are the catalyst for the theory about deferrals he develops as a teen.

- Tommy's first talk with Miss Lucy raises questions which lead him and Kathy to speculate about the purpose of the Gallery: 'Why did she bring it up? She's talking about you and you not creating. Then suddenly she starts up about this other stuff. What's the link? Why did she bring up donations? What's that got to do with you being creative?' (Kathy, p.30).
- Miss Lucy challenges some of the creating ideology but later reinforces the existence and importance of the Gallery: 'Tommy, I made a mistake…' 'Your art, it *is* important. And not just because it's evidence' (pp.105–6).
- Unanswered questions and Tommy's trusting nature lead to his theory about the Gallery's role in acquiring a deferral: 'Don't forget Kath, what she's got reveals our souls' (p.173).

Paragraph 3: Learning the truth about Hailsham shatters everything Tommy believes.

- Miss Emily crushes all Tommy's beliefs and hopes when she admits the truth: 'Your life must now run the course that's been set for it' (p.261).
- Screaming in the field mirrors Tommy's childhood tantrums, implying a regression to his earlier state of despair: 'Tommy's figure, raging, shouting, flinging his fists and kicking out'; 'caked in mud and distorted with fury' (p.269).
- Tommy and Kathy's relationship suffers; their shared history was based on a lie so each other's presence now builds 'resentment' (p.272): 'more and more, Tommy tended to identify himself with the other donors at the centre' (p.271).

Sample conclusion

Tommy's character arc shows him evolve from an angry and insecure boy to a confident and humble man. His entire sense of self is built upon the belief that Hailsham students are special and that his life serves some greater purpose. His trust in the guardians never wavers, allowing their lies and deception to fuel his delusions and set him up for devastation. Even Miss Lucy, despite her attempts to help, perpetuates the illusory beliefs that lead Tommy to invest himself so deeply in his theory that his art can earn him and Kathy a deferral. All of this comes crashing down when the truth is revealed, resulting in Tommy losing everything that matters to him and eventually dying alone.

SAMPLE ANSWER

Examine the role of one symbol or motif in developing a theme or character.

Kazuo Ishiguro's *Never Let Me Go* explores ideas of power and freedom through the story of human clones who are bred to provide organs for transplants. Kathy, Tommy and Ruth are raised in a seemingly idyllic environment at Hailsham, cut off from the world. They are subjected to a deceptive system of control and indoctrinated into believing that sacrificing their lives is a privilege. Despite this, the desire for freedom and autonomy is never fully eradicated. After many years apart, the trio reunites on a trip to see a beached boat during a time in their lives when the inevitability of death is looming over them. The abandoned boat functions as a symbol of power and freedom, embodying both clones' alienation and their desire to control their fates.

On one level the boat symbolises the clones' exclusion by a society that does not value the dignity of their lives. The boat is stranded in the countryside, concealed by 'woods' that get darker the further the characters venture into them, which parallels how the clones were hidden away at Hailsham. The fact that the characters stumble across the boat suddenly when stepping into a 'clearing' symbolises how the clones are hidden in plain sight and people just want to pretend they don't exist to avoid having to admit their complicity in injustice. Described as an 'old fishing boat' that was likely abandoned by its owners, the boat represents how clones are perceived as objects to be discarded. However, this attitude is subverted by the serene mood evoked by the calm weather and 'pale sky', and Ruth calling the boat 'beautiful'. This undermines the clones' alienation, reminding readers that the clones are of more value than society deems them to be.

The boat also symbolises the clones' powerlessness and entrapment. Typically boats and water represent freedom, so the image of a boat stranded in stagnant water calls attention to the clones' inability to change their fate. Ideas about death and decay are evoked through details such as 'ghostly dead trunks', 'crumbling' wood and 'cracking' paint. This imagery emphasises the inevitability of death and passing time, which applies to all humans, but is made all the more tragic given that clones' deaths are the result of intentional acts of brutality. The inclusion of this scene at this point, when Kathy is a carer, Tommy is a donor and Ruth is dying, highlights how little time they have left. However, once again, the mood of the scene is oddly peaceful, suggesting the characters are facing their deaths with a dignified grace that represents their strength in the face of horrific repression.

The trip to see the boat is sparked by Ruth's impending death and represents a final attempt at controlling fate. While leaving the recovery centre and seeing the boat provide Ruth a moment of joy and respite, her true motivation is to reunite Kathy and Tommy. On the trip home she apologises for all the ways she has hurt Kathy and Tommy, implying a desire for absolution in the face of death. Going to the effort of finding Madame's address and giving it to Tommy and Kathy so they can seek a deferral also shows her desire for them to have more time and a taste of a normal life. It is an act driven by the desire to believe 'it's not too late' for the people Ruth loves most to have a 'real chance' at happiness. As the catalyst for this trip, the boat symbolises Ruth's need to believe some kind of freedom is possible, even if it is too late for her.

Never Let Me Go presents a ruthless world that victimises innocent people in the most shocking ways. The clones have no control over their lives and are powerless to change their fate. The beached boat symbolises how the clones have been abandoned by society, pushed to the margins and robbed of all freedom, as well as being a visual reminder of the inescapable reality of death. However, it also symbolises the main characters' strength and courage. They remain hopeful in the face of atrocity, never giving up the will to live or to make the best of their circumstances. This is an empowering attitude that enables them to live their lives with dignity.

REFERENCES & READING

Text

Ishiguro, K 2005a, *Never Let Me Go*, Faber, London.

Film

Never Let Me Go 2010, dir. Mark Romanek, DNA Films and Film4 Productions. Starring Carey Mulligan, Keira Knightley and Andrew Garfield.

References and further reading

Adams, T 2005, 'For me, England is a mythical place' [Interview with Kazuo Ishiguro], *The Guardian*, 20 February, https://www.theguardian.com/books/2005/feb/20/fiction.kazuoishiguro

Barr, NA et al. 2022, 'United Kingdom', *Encyclopedia Britannica,* https://www.britannica.com/place/United-Kingdom

Barrow, A 2005, '*Never Let Me Go* by Kazuo Ishiguro – Artist of a floating world', *The Independent*, 25 February, https://www.independent.co.uk/arts-entertainment/books/reviews/never-let-me-go-by-kazuo-ishiguro-746328.html

Blackford, R 2016, 'Dolly the Sheep and the human cloning debate — twenty years later', *The Conversation*, 9 August, https://theconversation.com/dolly-the-sheep-and-the-human-cloning-debate-twenty-years-later-63712

Film Independent 2010, 'Kazuo Ishiguro discusses his intention behind writing the novel, *Never Let Me Go*', YouTube, 11 September, https://www.youtube.com/watch?v=_jCB59pPG7k

Fuller, S 2017, 'Posthumanism', in BS Turner (ed.), *The Wiley-Blackwell Encyclopedia of Social Theory*, Wiley Online Library, https://onlinelibrary.wiley.com/doi/epdf/10.1002/9781118430873.est0282

Grudin, R 2022, 'Humanism', *Encyclopedia Britannica*, https://www.britannica.com/topic/humanism

Harrison, MJ 2005, 'Clone alone', *The Guardian*, 27 February, https://www.theguardian.com/books/2005/feb/26/bookerprize2005.bookerprize

Hern, A 2017, 'Give robots "personhood" status, EU committee argues', *The Guardian*, 13 January, https://www.theguardian.com/technology/2017/jan/12/give-robots-personhood-status-eu-committee-argues

Ishiguro, K 2005b, 'Author Q&A', Penguin Random House, https://www.penguinrandomhouse.com/books/85609/never-let-me-go-by-kazuo-ishiguro/

Ishiguro, K 2017, 'Nobel Lecture', The Nobel Prize, https://www.nobelprize.org/prizes/literature/2017/ishiguro/lecture/

Lee, JE 2019, 'Norfolk and the Sense of Loss: The Bildungsroman and Colonial Subjectivity in Kazuo Ishiguro's *Never Let Me Go*', *Texas Studies in Literature and Language*, vol. 61, no. 3, pp. 270–90.

Levy, T 2011, 'Human Rights Storytelling and Trauma Narrative in Kazuo Ishiguro's *Never Let Me Go*', *Journal of Human Rights*, vol. 10, no. 1, pp.1–16.

Maleska, K 2019, 'Clones are humans: the dystopian elements in Kazuo Ishiguro's *Never Let Me Go*', *Journal of Contemporary Philology*, vol. 2, no. 1, pp. 123-38.

Mullan, J 2010,'On First Reading *Never Let Me Go*', in S Matthews & S Groes (eds), *Kazuo Ishiguro: Contemporary Critical Perspectives*, Bloomsbury Publishing, London, pp. 104–103.

NHGRI 2020, *Cloning Fact Sheet*, National Human Genome Research Institute, https://www.genome.gov/about-genomics/fact-sheets/Cloning-Fact-Sheet

Nobel Prize 2022, *The Nobel Prize in Literature 2017*, Nobel Prize, Nobel Prize Outreach AB, https://www.nobelprize.org/prizes/literature/2017/summary/

O'Keeffe, A 2017, 'Why serious literary fiction like Ishiguro's is vital in times like these', *The Guardian*, 7 October, https://www.theguardian.com/commentisfree/2017/oct/06/kazuo-ishiguro-nobel-prize-digital-age-serious-literary-fiction-vital

Rugnetta, M 2022, 'Cloning', *Encyclopedia Britannica,* https://www.britannica.com/science/cloning

Tait, A 2022, ' "I am, in fact, a person": can artificial intelligence ever be sentient?', *The Guardian*, 14 August, https://www.theguardian.com/technology/2022/aug/14/can-artificial-intelligence-ever-be-sentient-googles-new-ai-program-is-raising-questions

Tait, T 2005, 'A Sinister Harvest', *The Telegraph*, 13 March, https://www.telegraph.co.uk/culture/books/3638242/A-sinister-harvest.html

The Ethics Centre 2018, *Ethics Explainer: Post-Humanism*, The Ethics Centre, 22 February, https://ethics.org.au/ethics-explainer-post-humanism/

Vichiensing, M 2017, 'The Othering in Kazuo Ishiguro's *Never Let Me Go*', Advances in Language and Literary Studies, vol. 8, no. 4, pp.126–35.

Vorhaus, D 2007, 'Review of Kazuo Ishiguro, *Never Let Me Go*', *The American Journal of Bioethics*, vol. 7, no. 2, pp.99–100.

Wong, M 2018, 'Kazuo Ishiguro's "Never Let Me Go" Is a Masterpiece of Racial Metaphor', *Electric Literature*, 9 January, https://electricliterature.com/kazuo-ishiguros-never-let-me-go-is-a-masterpiece-of-racial-metaphor/

Wootson Jr, CR 2017, 'Saudi Arabia, which denies women equal rights, makes a robot a citizen', *The Washington Post*, 29 October, https://www.washingtonpost.com/news/innovations/wp/2017/10/29/saudi-arabia-which-denies-women-equal-rights-makes-a-robot-a-citizen/

Wroe, N 2005, 'Living memories', *The Guardian*, 19 February, https://www.theguardian.com/books/2005/feb/19/fiction.kazuoishiguro